R E
S D
V T J I H
U F
Q C G
B K X
A
WHERE WE KNOW: *New Orleans* AS HOME
P
N M

D1304541

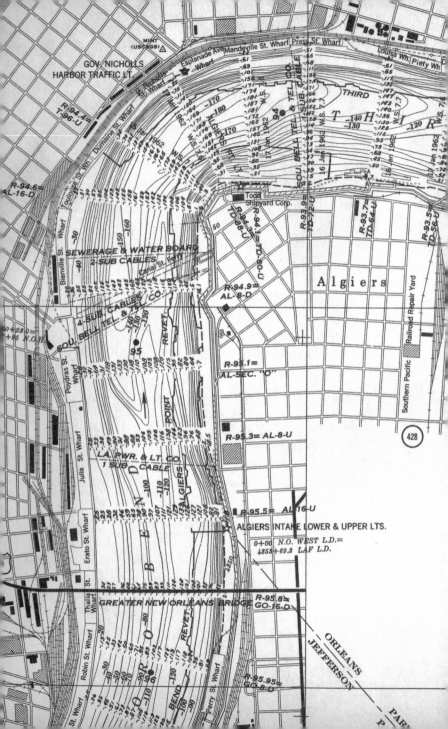

NEW ORLE

District
St. Pauline St. Wharf
Poland St. Wharf

INNER HARBOR NAVIGATION CANAL

FORSTALL ST. DISCHARGE LT.

DISTRICT
W. S. 7.6
W.S. 7.6
93

PBM 215 2

INNER HARBOR NAVIGATION CANAL LT. NO.

INNER HARBOR NAVIGATION CANAL LT. NO. 2

REACH

W. S. 8.0
W. S. 8.0
W. S.

C E N T R A L

R E A C H

PBM DRY DOCKS

Dry Dock

Dry Dock

157+74.0=
158+03.6C.S.

PBM 215 3

U.S. Naval
Reservation

R.91.7=
TD-8-D

PBM 215 4

O R L E A N S

P A R I S H,

LEE
(USC&GS)

UGE
ton's Ferry
Colyell
Springs
Springfield
Poncha
toula
T
Madison
Alligator v.
Port Vincent
Bayou Barbary
Manchac
French Set
Clio
Maurepas
St. Amant
Head of Isl
Lake
Maurepas
Whitehall
River
NSION
PONTCH
Blind River
Burnside
JAMES
Mt. Airy
Bonnet Carre
Frenier
Spanish
Houmas
Convent
St. Peter
St.JOHN BAPTIST
La Place
La Branche
West E
Burnside
Lemy's
Edgard
Hester
Johnson
Sarpys
Welcome
St. Patrick
Star
Pecan Gr.
Vacherie
Dugan
Hahnville
Luling
R. Davis
Boutte
CHARLES
R. Waggaman
Westwego
Andesville
marle
ke. Des Allemands
Des
Allemand
Lake Boeuf
Rosseau
Ewing
PAC.
Raceland
Lake Jes
Barata
LaFourche
Salvador
Lockport
LA FOURCHE
Crescent
Lake Fields
Long Lake
uthdown
Houma

M E A N Y

Mande V Benton
Jc.

ridge
iba

Generally
Florenville
L.

Mandeville
combe

Pearl
River

Slidell

Guzman

N E W   O R L.

Gainesville

Bay St. Louis

Waveland

Toulme V.

NASH

Pearl
o Riv.

St. o

AIN

Aux Herbes
Aux Herbes

Fort Pike

Rigolets

English Look

Half Moon

Lake Catherine

Petite Pass
Isl.

Gentilly

E
LOUIS V.

A
N
S

Chef
Menteur

Alligator Pt.

Gran

Lea Micheaud

NEW ORLEANS Lake

Proctors Pt.

Borgne

Shalmette

Auburn

Saxonholm

M. G. Canal

Poydras

St. Bernard

S A I N T   B E R N A R D

English Toca

Turn

St. Clair

Stella

Reggio B.

Shell Beach

Hopedale

Greenwood

Belair

Monticello

Gordelet

Saint Sophie

Nero

A

Pt. Ch

L'Eloi

Bay

Grove

Junior

Lawrence

Grand Bayou

Diamono

Empire Mill

Bohemia

Pointe a la Hache

Pt. la Fortune

ISLE

Gran

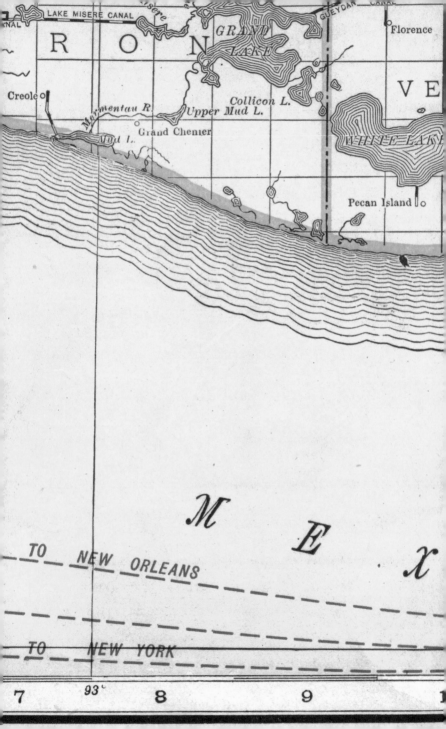

WHERE WE KNOW: **NEW ORLEANS** AS HOME

NEW ORLEANS
NEW-ORLEANS
NEW ORLEANS
New Orleans
NEW ORLEANS
New Orleans.
New Orleans
NEW ORLEANS
New Orleans
NEW ORLEANS
NEW ORLEANS
NEW ORLEANS
NEW ORLEANS
NEW ORLEANS
NEW ORLEANS
New Orleans

edited by **DAVID RUTLEDGE**

FALL 2010
BROKEN LEVEE BOOKS
an imprint of
CHIN MUSIC PRESS, *PUBLISHERS*
SEATTLE

PUBLISHER:
Chin Music Press
2621 24ᵗʰ AVE W
Seattle, WA 98199
USA

www.chinmusicpress.com

All rights reserved
ISBN: 978-0-9844576-1-8
A Broken Levee Book
Broken Levee Books is an imprint of Chin Music Press.
First {1} Edition
BOOK DESIGN: Joshua Powell
Printed by Imprimerie Gauvin, CANADA
Library of Congress Cataloging-in-Publication Data is available.

"Still Live, with Voices" by Lolis Eric Elie was previously published in
the *Oxford American* (Issue 62, "Three Years After: New Orleans & the
Gulf Coast — In Their Own Words")

"New Orleans Loss" by Eve Troeh aired as a radio essay on American
Public Media's "Weekend America" in January 2006.

Part of Eve Troeh's "Dear New Orleans" was broadcast on National
Public Radio's "All Things Considered" on August 28, 2007.

Photographs copyright Sandra Burshell.

"Plumage," an illustration by Matt Phelan, appears on pages 276-277.

To infuse this book with a New Orleanian soul, Josh Powell traveled to the
Crescent City, drank in Harry's Bar, ate pickled okra, threw up that okra about a
block from Brangelina's house, slept on an old and musty mattress in Professor
Rutledge's apartment, attended a *Treme* party, dined at Bayona, rifled through
hundreds of maps and prints at bookstores and libraries and stayed up till dawn at
least once.

For those who wish to come home – and those who we wish could come home

A

I am at length arrived in the famous City, which they have called
la nouvelle Orleans. Those who have given it this Name thought
that *Orleans* was of the feminine Gender: But what signifies that?
Custom has established it, and that is above the Rules of Grammar.

This City is the first, which one of the greatest Rivers in the World
has been raised on its Banks. If the eight Hundred fine Houses,
and the five Parishes, which the News-Papers gave it some two
Years ago, are reduced at present to a hundred Barracks, placed
in no very great Order; to a great Store-House, built of Wood; to
two or three Houses, which would be no Ornament to a Village of
France; and to the half of a sorry Store-House, which they agreed
to lend to the Lord of the Place, and which he had no sooner taken
Possession of, but they turned him out to dwell under a Tent; what
Pleasure, on the other Side, to see insensibly encreasing this future
Capital of a fine and vast Country, and to be able to say, not with
a Sigh, like the Hero of *Virgil*, speaking of his dear native Place
consumed by the Flames, and the Fields where *Troy* Town had
been, but full of a well grounded Hope, this wild and desart Place,
which the Reeds and Trees do yet almost wholly cover, will be one
Day, and perhaps the Day is not far off, an opulent City, and the
Metropolis of a great and rich Colony.

JANUARY 26

I have nothing to add to what I said in the Beginning of the former
Letter concerning the present State of *New Orleans.* The truest Idea
that you can form of it, is to represent to yourself two hundred
Persons that are sent to build a City, and who are encamped on
the Side of a great River, where they have thought of nothing but
to shelter themselves from the Injuries of the Air, whilst they wait

for a plan, and have built themselves Houses. M. *de Pauger*, whom I have still the Honour to accompany, has just now shewed me one of his drawing. It is very fine and very regular; but it will not be so easy to execute it, as it was to trace it on Paper.

PIERRE-FRANCOIS XAVIER DE CHARLEVOIX
(printed for R. Goadby, 1763)

B

SEPTEMBER 5, 1722

A man named Traverse, living in New Orleans, was let out of prison. This man had built a house in New Orleans. This house was not set in accord with the alignment of the streets, as he had built it before the plan had been proposed. M. Peauger [assistant to the chief engineer] had it torn down. Traverse being not well pleased about this, presented a petition to the council, asking them to recompense him for his house in order that he might have the means to build another. M. Peauger had him sent for, and, after having regaled him with a volley of blows with his stick, had him thrown into prison, with irons about his feet, and today this man has come out of prison almost blind …

SEPTEMBER 12

Toward ten o'clock in the evening there sprang up the most terrible hurricane which has been seen in these quarters. At New Orleans thirty-four houses were destroyed as well as sheds, including the church, the parsonage and the hospital. In the hospital were some people sick with wounds. All the other houses were damaged about the roofs or walls…

It is to be remarked that if the Mississipy had been high this hurricane would have put both banks of the river more than 15 feet under water, the Mississipy, although low, having risen 8 feet…

SEPTEMBER 14

We are working hard here to repair the damage which the
hurricane has caused …

DIRON D'ARTAGUIETTE
(translated by Newton D. Mereness, 1916)

CONTENTS

xxiii   Introduction

H O M E   002   Anne Gisleson, *Reconstruction Baby*

    008   Sarah Inman, *The Gutting*

    025   Kris Lackey, *Ghostland Sublime*

    035   A short story by Ray Shea, *Gather the Fragments that Remain*

C U L T U R E &   049   Lolis Eric Elie, *Still Live, with Voices*

H I S T O R Y   059   Barbara Bodichon, *A Dull Life* (1867)

    075   Charles Dudley Warner, *New Orleans* (1887)

    098   Sam Jasper, *Triangular Sound Bites*

    107   David Rutledge, *On Terence Blanchard*

    123   A short story by Rex Noone, *Asides on the Tuba*

    131   Reggie Poché, *When We Make a Feast: Food as Prayer at the New Orleans Table*

    147   Rebecca Freeland-Hebert, *Tattooing Katrina*

L O S S   167   Sandra Burshell, *After Katrina*

    176   Mark Folse, *In the Brown Zone with Mother Cabrini*

    184   Jennifer Kuchta, *Jennie's Grocery: R.I.P.*

    192   Sarah DeBacher, *We Live on Both Sides*

    198   Sam Jasper, *Breach of Contract*

    200   Tracey Tangerine, *In My Face*

    206   Eve Troeh, *New Orleans Loss*

H O M E I !   212   Mark Folse, *Carry Me Home*

    220   Eve Troeh, *Dear New Orleans: I'm Leaving You*

    228   Eve Abrams, *Borrowed Time*

    239   Ray Shea, *In My Home Over There*

    254   Ali Arnold, *For Now*

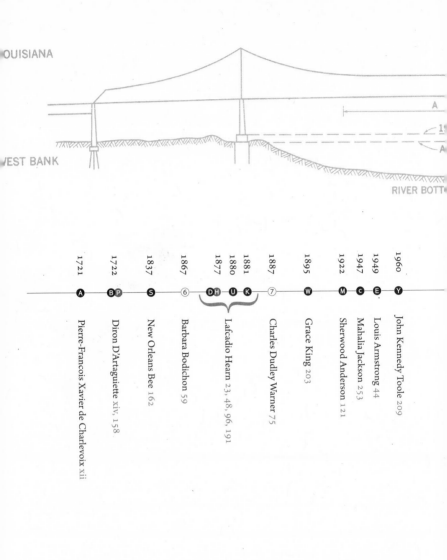

LOUISIANA

WEST BANK

RIVER BOTTOM

1721   Ⓐ   Pierre-François Xavier de Charlevoix xii

1722   ⒷⓅ   Diron D'Artaguiette xiv, 158

1837   Ⓢ   New Orleans Bee 162

1867   ⑥   Barbara Bodichon 59

1877
1880   ⒹⒽ ⓊⓀ   Lafcadio Hearn 23, 48, 96, 191
1881

1887   ⑦   Charles Dudley Warner 75

1895   Ⓦ   Grace King 203

1922   Ⓜ   Sherwood Anderson 121

1947   Ⓒ   Mahalia Jackson 253

1949   Ⓔ   Louis Armstrong 44

1960   Ⓨ   John Kennedy Toole 209

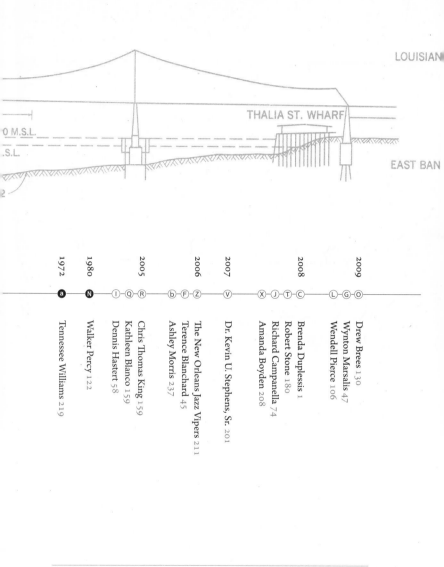

LOUISIAN

THALIA ST. WHARF

0 M.S.L.

.S.L.

EAST BAN

1972 — Tennessee Williams 219

1980 — Walker Percy 122

2005 — Chris Thomas King 159
Kathleen Blanco 159
Dennis Hastert 58

2006 — The New Orleans Jazz Vipers 211
Terence Blanchard 45
Ashley Morris 237

2007 — Dr. Kevin U. Stephens, Sr. 201

2008 — Brenda Duplessis 1
Robert Stone 180
Richard Campanella 74
Amanda Boyden 208

2009 — Drew Brees 130
Wynton Marsalis 47
Wendell Pierce 106

When We Know: A CHRONOLOGICAL
REFERENCE TO
QUOTATIONS FEATURED
IN THIS VOLUME

Anne Gisleson, *Reconstruction Baby* ❶ **Bywater/Upper Ninth**

Sarah Inman, *The Gutting* ❷ **Gentilly** (on Rocheblave, just
East of Elysian Fields)

Kris Lackey, *Ghostland Sublime* ❸ **Gentilly**

Barbara Bodichon, *A Dull Life* ❹ **Carrollton**

Sam Jasper, *Triangular Sound Bites* ❺ **Marigny**

Rex Noone, *Asides on the Tuba* ❻ **French Quarter**

Reggie Poché, *When We Make a Feast:* ❼ **Garyville, LA**/St. Louis, MO
Food as Prayer at the New Orleans Table

Mark Folse, *In the Brown Zone* ❽ **Gentilly** (St. Francis Cabrini Catholic
with Mother Cabrini Church, in the Vista Park section of
Gentilly along Paris Avenue)

Jennifer Kuchta, *Jennie's Grocery: R.I.P.* ❾ **Touro** (3700 Magazine Street)

Sarah DeBacher, *We Live on Both Sides* ❿ **Holy Cross**

Eve Troeh, *New Orleans Loss* ⓫ **Marigny**

Mark Folse, *Carry Me Home* ⓬ **Marigny**/Fargo, ND

Eve Troeh, *Dear New Orleans:* ⓭ Los Angeles, CA
I'm Leaving You

Eve Abrams, *Borrowed Time* ⓮ **Bywater**

Ray Shea, *In My Home Over There* ⓯ **Treme**

Ali Arnold, *For Now* ⓰ **Bywater**

Where We Know: LOCATING THE ESSAYS
AND STORIES IN THIS
VOLUME

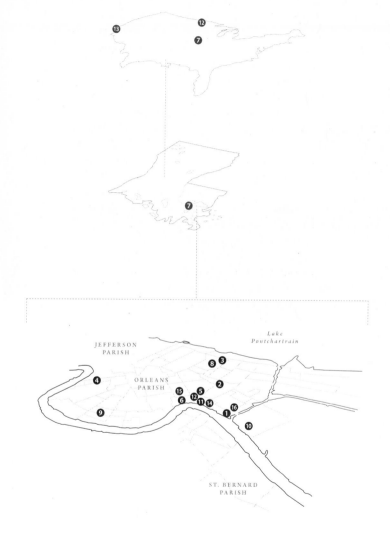

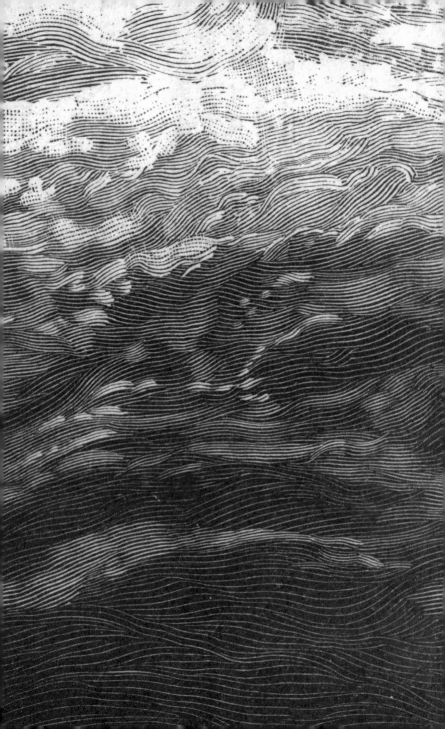

History continues in New Orleans. Even after the cameras — the news cameras, the tourist cameras — New Orleanians find themselves living through history each day. The decision to rebuild or to demolish a house; the choice to leave one's home or to gut and try again; the culture and the traditions that make living here so rewarding, even as we face unprecedented challenges; the constant promise of this city: these are historical circumstances, these are current circumstances. These are among the topics one will find in this book.

Introduction

Then there are those days when one tries to return to "the Big Easy," that dream of what this city once was, even if living here never really was so "easy." These are the days when one tries to forget the immediate past, to forget the pressing concerns of today, to celebrate Mardi Gras or Jazz Fest, to put aside the problems one has with one's house, one's insurance, one's escalating rent. One's dysfunctional city. On those days, too, history imposes itself: there is rarely a day when the situation of our city can truly be put out of mind. But the precarious nature of our place can intensify time, as Eve Abrams shows in her essay "Borrowed Time."

That deeper understanding of time can lend itself to some excellent celebrations. Perhaps that is one reason why, historically, this city has been so much better at celebrations than any other American city.

If life in New Orleans has never been "easy," as I hope this book will show, it has also been — more often than not — worth the effort.

This is not to say that those who have decided to leave New Orleans — decided that this city is no longer home — are wrong. These are wrenching decisions: to stay or not to stay, to rebuild or not. To risk the next hurricane or not. To trust one's life, one's future, one's family to the Army Corps of Engineers. To live with the possibility of violence that has become so much a part of life in New Orleans. These are decisions that should not come easily. Eve Troeh's two essays in this anthology articulate this sense in a very clear and perhaps disturbing manner.

History continues here as we face situations that the rest of the country will face soon, if they have not faced them already: the decay of American infrastructure; the ruin of the American environment — or, more specifically, the ruin that corporations have left of the American environment; the breakdown of American cities; the blunt fact of American poverty and the attempts by some business-minded leaders to sweep that poverty out of view, off to another city if the opportunity (ie, a national disaster) presents itself. Health care on the ropes, schools in need of redefinition. Big parties that are still a whole lot of fun.

Oops, in good New Orleanian tradition, my list switched. This city is never wholly negative. We face these issues with some hope or, when that hope seems naïve, we throw one hell of a party.

Every celebrant feels that he or she lives only in the moment, but even the festivals of this city are linked to history. Visitors may drive down from elsewhere to get drunk and to witness the spectacle; they have unknowingly driven into history, submerged themselves in the past. Their awareness — or lack thereof — is irrelevant: history surrounds them. They are in it.

Some cities do what they can to eliminate history, tearing down old structures in the name of progress, replacing them with the more "progressive" structures of corporate America. By working toward progress in this manner, this ahistorical manner, they impoverish the present, depriving it of depth. Of course, New Orleans has not been immune to this process, not by any means. Louis Armstrong's home is nowhere for us to visit. There are certainly times when the decision to save or replace the past is problematic. Here, however, there is more of a tendency not only to preserve the past, but to live alongside of it, to live in the midst of it. Our history is not for the museums. We still have a culture that comes from the city, from the neighborhoods; we still have a culture that connects to the past and parades in the streets.

In 1842 a man named Charles Powell commented that "unlike the cities of the north, street music is tolerated in New Orleans." (Thanks to Richard Campanella's *Bienville's Dilemma* — p. 265 — for pointing that one out.)

That other kind of culture — the kind that we must continually resist — comes from above, but it does not trickle down: it stomps down — with a large footprint — erasing whatever remnants of local culture may get in its way. One needs only to look at any American city to see this. One needs only to look at New Orleans to learn that this kind of culture flees town and does little or nothing to help rebuild after a disaster. Don't count on McDonald's to anchor your neighborhood when it is in need. Don't count on Starbucks. Corporate culture has no connection to home. If you are about to purchase this book at the Border's on St. Charles Street, I want you to put it down and go to Octavia Books or the Garden District Book Shop or Faulkner House Books. Your local culture awaits in a neighborhood nearby. Go explore Beckham's Book Shop in the French Quarter.

That culture from above — that corporate culture — renders the ghosts of the past nearly inaudible, leading some to believe that such ghosts do not even exist.

Here we know better. Here we — or a great many of us — revere the culture. Here we listen to our ghosts, even offering tours to point out some of their more notorious locations. I would note, though, that not all ghosts are loud enough to attract tourists. Many of them are quiet and only communicate with residents. I suggest a new bumper sticker: Protect the Ghosts.

Some of the writers in this anthology look at the problematic changes taking place in this city. Sarah DeBacher's piece, "We Live on Both Sides," shows the concerns that can come about when neighborhoods change for the most benevolent of reasons. Jennifer Kuchta's "Jennie's Grocery: R.I.P." conveys the nostalgia that one may have for places of the past, even if those places were not the greatest of neighbors. Ray Shea looks hard at the irrecoverable in his moving "In My Home Over There." New Orleans, to put it lightly, is in a time of transition. For what it is worth, though, there have been many times of transition in its past, and many times when the culture felt threatened.

After the Louisiana Purchase, locals felt the encroachment of American interests, an influx of English-speaking people who were a threat to the local culture. One concern was whether Mardi Gras could survive the excess presence of Protestants; in 1846, Charles Lyell wrote of "the violent shock which the invasion of the Anglo-Americans is about to give to the old régime of Louisiana." After the Civil War, northern and federal interests moved in for the business and political opportunities, and once again local life felt threatened. In 1880, Lafcadio Hearn wrote a piece for the New Orleans newspaper *The Daily City Item*, entitled "The Pelican's Ghost." In this piece the state bird laments the loss of a culture, declaring that he has passed away because New Orleans has become "Americanized." You will find that article in these pages.

Still, the culture is resilient, and the outsider who comes to New Orleans is often transformed for good. I speak from experience.

Charles Dudley Warner, writing for *Harper's New Monthly Magazine*, expressed this same idea in 1887: "To the Northern stranger the aspect and manners of the city are foreign, but if he remains long enough he is sure to yield to its fascinations, and become a partisan of it." In that same article, entitled "New Orleans," Warner also wrote: "… it is a city of the past, and specially interesting in its picturesque decay." This sounds similar to the setting that Tennessee Williams provides for *A Streetcar Named Desire* (1947), where the "tender blue" New Orleans sky "gracefully attenuates the atmosphere of decay." How is it that a city can maintain an atmosphere of graceful decay for so many decades?

Perhaps that constant sense of threat — of decay, of weather, of being "Americanized" — is exactly what has caused so many to rally around the culture of this city, as if protecting something under siege. Perhaps that sense of threat has led to preservation. Although, I must admit, the word "preservation" is too suggestive of a museum; it does not do justice to the living thing that the culture of New Orleans continues to be. That culture-under-siege is surviving; at times, it even feels like it is thriving. This story of resilience is one that America needs: culture can still be something connected to

home, something one lives, not merely a product one pur-
chases or a program one tunes in to watch. The culture of
New Orleans is no place for the sedentary.

This city has plenty of lessons for the rest of the country.

America should be paying attention, but most of the cameras left while we were in the midst of recovery, as viewers
— or perhaps, more often, producers — expressed "fatigue"
toward our suffering. As though they needed a less difficult
story to keep them entertained. CNN, of course, obliged,
along with the rest of the networks. That shortsightedness
— that short attention span — may come back to haunt the
country. Rather than changing the channel, America should
be learning the lessons of New Orleans.

America needs New Orleans more than we need America.

As I write this introduction, the pelicans are threatened
again, literally this time. The oil is pouring into the gulf, leaving residents of the region uncertain and disconsolate. We let
a reckless child play in our backyard with no supervision. The
uncertainty of that threat in the gulf — that looming presence gaining in destructive strength each day — makes it feel
like a bad sequel. (That first show — Katrina — was so popular, after all.) The cameras are back. The faces on TV are once
again paying attention to us. We know, however, that those
cameras are only temporary, that our area just happens to be
the big story once again. We know that we will be left alone to
deal with the full implications of the story.

BP's pathetic attempts at stopping the seemingly endless
supply of oil (with top hats and junk shots) is only making
them look increasingly incompetent. If this were fiction, it
would be an allegory. Unfortunately, it is all-too-real, and our
region has to face another threat. As of publication, we have
no idea how extensive the damage will be or how many years
it will take to recover or if "recovery" will be possible. We do

not know how permanent this damage might be.

I want to add many angry adjectives to the two previous paragraphs. By the time this book is published, we might know which adjectives are appropriate and where they belong. On the other hand, this anger — the region's anger and currently flowing beyond this region — might remain raw and unrefined for some time.

To put it mildly, this region has had its share of disasters. All of this adds to the already-complex topic of living in New Orleans.

THIS BOOK IS ABOUT THE choice of making — or not making — New Orleans one's home. This is not a post-Katrina book any more than New Orleans is a post-Katrina city. The story of New Orleans is much more than that; the stories of New Orleans are much more than that.

There are a series of bumper stickers that every New Orleanian knows, based on the first one which states, "New Orleans: Proud to Call It Home." Since that original, there have been several variations: "New Orleans: Proud to Crawl Home," and, after the levee breaks, "New Orleans: Proud to Swim Home."

Recently I saw one in Spanish: "Nueva Orleans: Con Orgullo Vivimos Aquí." It is interesting that the Spanish version is more communal, stating "vivimos" ("we live"), as though informing those driving behind that a new group has established itself in the city. This version also eliminates the word "home," referring merely to "here" ("aquí"); perhaps many of the recent Latino arrivals to Nueva Orleans are undecided as to whether or not this city will be a true home.

Paul Hayes, a bartender at Harry's in the Quarter, suggested a title for this book: "New Orleans: Proud It Called

Me Home." That could be the title for some of the pieces in this book. For other voices represented here, the statement is not so simple. Not everyone is so proud and not everyone remained "home." This, too, has a historical resonance: in past years, people as closely associated with New Orleans as Louis Armstrong and Walker Percy have, at some point, rejected life in this city.

I have also heard of — but have not seen — this idea for that line of bumper stickers: "New Orleans: Proud to Call It Quits."

In fact, this book would best be represented by an ambitious car owner who chose to put all of those stickers on a car, even the contradictory ones. It would be a busy bumper, indeed, but it would reflect the reality of this city.

New Orleans is, to say the least, a problematic home. It is also a rewarding one. As with our previous anthology, *Do You Know What It Means to Miss New Orleans?*, this book celebrates a resilient city and the culture that cannot be kept down. As Wynton Marsalis points out, it is culture that gives one's life integrity. It is culture, ultimately, that makes New Orleans meaningful. It is culture that makes it home.

Residents of this city express that sense of home in a variety of ways. Rebecca Freeland-Hebert's project, accompanied by the photography of Sandra Burshell, shows that the passion of home can by conveyed by a tattoo. You will see those tattoos — and read about the reasons behind them — in these pages.

The writers included in this book are all concerned, in a variety of ways, with what New Orleans means. Whether it is Sam Jasper listening to the many sounds of the Marigny or Ray Shea making Willie Mae's fried chicken seem irresistible, each writer in this anthology shows something significant about this culture. Rex Noone will take you into the troubled mind of an aspiring tuba player. Lolis Eric Elie will take you through the complex history of the city. Sarah Inman will provide the details of housegutting. Not only in their writing, but in their lives, each of the writers in this anthology is concerned with what it means to make New Orleans home. Ali Arnold writes of her love for the city even as she thinks of a day when she will no longer be here.

These are complex times for the culture of New Orleans, and this book makes no claims toward being complete. In fact, it is difficult to keep up with this "easy" city: while I was putting together this anthology, the Saints won the Super Bowl — allowing for one of the most euphoric moods the city has ever seen — and, months later, BP's endless deluge brought morale back down. New Orleans exists in a continual rhythm of raised spirits and recovery. The opening passages of this book — from 1721 and 1722 — also show that pattern. Those who live in New Orleans must adjust to such fluctuations; often, we can find life in them.

The post-flood photographs by Sandra Burshell show that beauty can be found within the devastation. That idea might be surprising to some people. Ralph Waldo Emerson wrote, "There is no object so foul that intense light will not make beautiful." I have often wondered if this is true; her photographs lend evidence to the idea that it is. The artist's eye can redeem a disaster.

Perhaps.

There could be a book on the displaced people of our city and how they are coping with another culture, perhaps striving to maintain some sense of home in a new city. The incompetence of BP may add to the number of displaced people. But that is another book. *Where We Know* stays inside of the city, and shows some of the parallels between historical and current accounts of this place; it will swerve through the past, back to the present, commenting on and contemplating the topic of New Orleans. The result, we hope, is to convey some of the poetry of home.

DAVID RUTLEDGE
New Orleans
August 2010

EXPLANATORY

Spelling in this book may appear to be inconsistent. That is because we are staying true to the original texts. "Mississipy" is not a mistake; "Toulane" is not a mistake. At least, they are not our mistakes. Our purpose here is not to correct spelling or grammar or to push each voice into conforming to some standard. Our purpose is to respect each voice, along with each quirky spelling, non-standard grammar and any other method of expression.

PART ONE
Home.

"We've been running since Katrina, scared, panicking, about everything that's going on in New Orleans with the flood and the water and the hurricanes. It make us disgusted, depressed, and everything else.

It's really not worth staying in New Orleans, but that's where we from. That's where we know."

Brenda Duplessis, an evacuee in Conway, Arkansas, during hurricane Gustav, on KATV news, Little Rock, September 1, 2008

"Digger, digger!" the boys often point out from the backseat. My husband and I wouldn't have noticed the almost insidious appearance of these machines in and around the city had it not been for our two sons continually bringing them to our attention. But what we *have* noted, driving around these past few years, after the dreamy shock of the disaster began to wear off, is how stuff keeps disappearing. Buildings, whole blocks, shopping centers. A neat, complete sort of removal, leaving a raked-over plot of dirt or square of weeds and a questioning sensation—was that drugstore/bank/shotgun/Victorian mansion really ever there?

Reconstruction Baby

ANNE GISLESON

But the Reconstruction is loads of entertainment for our vehicularly obsessed two-year-old Otto, and his enthusiasm has rekindled a male toddler's primitive preoccupation with machinery in his nine-year-old brother Silas. Otto can identify a variety of trucks: diggers, front loaders, bulldozers, dump trucks, cement mixers, cranes. And not just from his little baby's-first-truck-books. Where we live, in the Bywater neighborhood of the Upper Ninth Ward, there are perfect spots to park the stroller and watch the dusty parade of construction traffic heading down St. Claude Avenue towards the once-breached Industrial Canal and the massive rebuilding zones of the Lower Ninth Ward and St. Bernard Parish.

Lately the Bywater, a 19th century mixed-industrial neighborhood along the Mississippi River, is full of such wonders. In the days immediately following the levee breaks, a huge warehouse fire broke out at the end of our street. The fire burned upriver for days, leaving six blocks of wharves destroyed. We lived with the wreckage for the last couple years until finally the massive, tangled ruins were cleared. Now, in our strolls around the neighborhood, the boys are treated to unobstructed views of the enormous cargo ships (*Boat, mom! Big boat!*) passing a few hundred yards away. This new topography of our neighborhood has also revealed a view of the soaring Mississippi River Bridge, which Otto can pick out over the shotgun houses and oak trees with great delight. These days, in a perverse sort of way, it's not hard to feel that much has been opened up to us.

Parenthood and the hurricane arrived for me at more or less the same moment. My husband Brad and I had barely unpacked from our Mexican honeymoon when we packed up six-year-old Silas, his son, whose birth mother had died a couple years before, and evacuated New Orleans at the last minute. I had never left for a hurricane in my life and initially had been determined to stay. Finally Brad saw that this particular hurricane did look kind of bad and that he would take Silas, and if I wanted to stay behind with a neighbor, I could. My choice. I had married a patient, reasonable and open man and for a couple hours that was the plan. But as I watched Brad load the car and prepare Silas, I realized it was time to mom-up and made my first real decision as a parent. So this is what it meant to be a mother, I thought begrudgingly, doing something you absolutely did not want to do for the sake of the family unit. But I did not do it gracefully. That afternoon I drank a bottle of white wine as I cooked up all the meat in the fridge, lamented my loss of independence, made us late with petty domestic chores and pouted the whole ride up to Tuscaloosa, even as the water pushed up over the oyster shell shoulder of Highway 11, harassing the pilings of the doomed fishing camps.

As the levees broke and the city was filling up with water, it occurred to me that I might be pregnant. Hours later, after a blurry trip to the drugstore, I sat stunned by the affirmative news in the bright light of the bathroom at the Red Roof Inn in Houston as Brad watched CNN churn out the unthinkable, Silas' sweet thin form asleep in the other double bed. The day before, we had driven over to Houston from Tuscaloosa along the I-20 corridor, swerving around downed trees and watching caravans of linemen from all over the country exit south towards the city. NPR kept telling us it would be weeks before they pumped the water out. We kept losing the station, and Silas, who has a kind of high-functioning autism and gets into obsessive, repetitive loops, hadn't stopped talking about the Berenstain Bears since we crossed into Mississippi. Hungry for news, raw and despairing, I had another little selfish unmotherly meltdown about whether or not I could handle this situation. After decades of being a self-involved single person, I didn't have a reserve of maternal patience to draw from.

Unmoored from any sense of a regular domestic life, flush with FEMA money and uncertainty, we kept heading West, me wanting to hit every Dairy Queen between Austin and L.A. to keep the nausea at bay. As we drove through the arid and intact Southwest, I began home-schooling Silas, who would've been repeating kindergarten that fall, in the backseat, working through phonics and number patterns. The first week of October our mayor told us he could smell the beignets cooking, that it was okay to come home. So we did. When we returned to the city, which was wrecked beyond all our imaginings, we were undoubtedly a family, forged in the confines of travel (car, motel, highway) by a kind of clutching love and refugee freedom.

Nearly eight months after the levees broke, I found myself in the Touro Infirmary where most of my family was born, blind with pain and curled into a ball, ready for the epidural. The nurse holding my shoulders alternately admonished me to focus and recounted to the anesthesiologist, who had just moved back to town and was about insert a needle between my vertebrae, that she'd only gotten thirty-thousand dollars for her destroyed house in Bay St. Louis. No moment was sacred from the storm's narrative. Touro had lost some staff and had hired on staff that had lost their hospitals. Everyone there had suffered, was still suffering, but neither that, nor the nature of their profession seemed to dampen their obvious pleasure in the aiding of a miracle, of welcoming Otto, an eighth-generation New Orleanian, to his broken but remarkable home.

Today, after the usual first-son trepidation, Silas has become a wonderful, dedicated older brother. His solid foundation of backseat phonics-training has served him well and he now reads to Otto with such enthusiasm and animation it's hard to believe that he's supposed to be affect-challenged. The search-and-rescue marks on houses and calls for help painted on the streets have faded into his visual vernacular, are no longer worthy of his attention. The debris piles and spent MRE packets we used to routinely pass on our stroller walks and scooter rides are all but gone. The hulking humvees patrolling our neighborhood are fewer and fewer, which I think is actually a disappointment for the boys, who once got candy handed to them from one as though we lived in Kabul.

Sure, fear and frustration, child-care issues and crime, still pervade everyday life. The government perennially disappoints and there is a lot of work to do. We're busy and tired — go to too many meetings, volunteer too much, pay too much in insurance and taxes and utilities and are aging around the eyes a little more quickly than we'd like. But the city is alive in a new sort of way, overtaken by unprecedented civic engagement and activity. It's suddenly gone from laid-back, funky port town a few beats behind the rest of the country to being a Petri dish for urban renewal and experimentation, leaving us natives excited and confused. New Orleans used to hemorrhage its best and brightest, but now young people are moving here in droves to be a part of the Historic Reconstruction, to partake in some exotic fieldwork without the passports and shots. There's a sense of hope, opportunity and purpose I never felt growing up here. Though sometimes it's strange raising children in a city so changed from the one we grew up in, given our city's history, and that we now have an opportunity to make it better, that's not an entirely bad thing. And I wonder what kind of memories are taking root in Silas and Otto, how they'll end up perceiving things.

Living in the city of your childhood, surrounded by family and places from your past, it's easy to slip into former states of yourself. Playing with your children on the same City Park oaks you once swung from, joshing around with your brothers and sisters in the kitchen before dinner at your folks' or running into someone from high school you haven't seen in years on Canal Street and without missing a beat you're cataloguing loss and talking about an old biology teacher. But now here we are, us, as adults, smack in the middle of History, charged with this important task, to not screw things up as badly as has been done in the past. For a lot of us rebuilding the city is inextricable from rebuilding ourselves, an attempt to lace the best of our lost childhoods to the better ones we want so badly for our own children. And here they are, watching it happen from backseats all over town, the tearing down and hopefully, soon, the building back up.

A stale moldy stink constricts my throat as I enter our friend Kim's house in Gentilly. It's a cute two bedroom, one-and-a-half bathroom with a modest yard, a driveway and a garage out back. Most of the homes in this neighborhood are just that — modest. The streets sit wider here than they do in our ward, and at the corner of St. Roch, there's a fenced-in field complete with a tattered swing set and monkey bars, a playground named the Saint James Playspot. About a year ago, my husband and I began looking at houses in this neighborhood, knowing that they were affordable. We'd go for rides on Sundays, stopping at "for sale" and "open house" signs. We

The Gutting*

SARAH INMAN
for Eric Martin

looked too for wheelchair ramps, an indication not of older folks but of people who had been shot and were now confined to wheelchairs. Good blocks have no houses with wheelchair ramps, but finding a part of New Orleans that hasn't been plagued by violence is almost impossible. Parts of Jefferson Parish and the North Shore can be cautiously viewed as low crime, and yet, if we ever want that kind of danger-free, flavorless lifestyle, we'll get better paying jobs and move far away from here.

Kim lived in her house on St. Roch for about a year and a

half before Katrina hit and the levees failed. Today, two days after Christmas, we drive across town to Gentilly. We come to help gut Kim's house, which took on, depending on which insurance adjustor she speaks with, between three-and-a-half feet to five feet of water after one of the levees broke. The water's height is a small discrepancy, considering that her home was submerged in the filthy fluid for almost a month. When we arrive, about a half a dozen people we normally see in the halls of the university, at bars, or at cocktail parties work to rip up buckled baseboard and tear away water-weary walls. I'm dressed in my worst — ripped jeans stained with paint and pitch, a stinky old t-shirt, a baseball cap and Timberland boots. I sense the importance of good footwear. Others are dressed similarly, in old jeans and t-shirts. Rachel, a newly divorced redhead and friend of Kim, wears a "Make Levees, Not War" t-shirt as if those of us who come today need to be reminded of the politics of the situation.

The ceiling in Kim's bedroom looks like a Palomino's hide, spotted with different shades of mold — green, black, yellow, gray. I'm not sure ponies have this many colors.

I get instructions from Bill, the academic administrator/poet/contractor who escaped the city in dramatic fashion after Katrina passed. (Who believes only the stupid and poor didn't leave?) Bill supervises the volunteers, mostly from the English department at the University of New Orleans, where my husband teaches. Bill points out some cypress baseboard that can be salvaged, so I slip a paper mask over my nose and mouth, grab tools, and go to work, trying to pry the cypress strip from the wall. The floorboards make it a difficult task, so I hack at those first. I work on one side of the room while Inge, a sinewy, redheaded Austrian and the director of the English learning lab, and Elizabeth, a newly retained instructor, rip up the other side. Elizabeth has dark curls, and today

9

her pleasant-looking smile is hidden behind a mask. They work as a team, Inge using a large pick ax to loosen a piece of the floorboard, and Elizabeth prying it free with a crowbar.

With a crowbar and hammer, I work carefully. I start to remove loose pieces of the floor near the cypress baseboard, but after yanking apart a few strips of hardwood, I find the cypress still will not budge. I switch to the center of the room and with each slate of floorboard that comes loose, I move closer to the wall to get at that baseboard. As I rip up the floor, I notice pages from books imprinted into the hardwood. Is it a page from a literature anthology or from a book on composition? Does it matter? How useful is subject-verb agreement now? Who cares about Kafka? As the muscles in my forearms, neck, legs and back tighten, that last stubborn strip of hardwood finally comes loose. I need my whole body for this job. Once I rip the last board from the floor, I then can pry the cypress baseboard away from the wall in one solid piece. It's a small task that takes me all morning to complete.

OTHER FRIENDS OF OURS, Neil and Eric moved last October to their bungalow in Lakeview. We know Justin and Elise enjoyed their Mid-City double shotgun for a little over two years, and Andrea and her family hadn't quite lived in Gentilly a year. (It wasn't such a good year for them. About three months before the hurricane, a neighborhood crack addict broke into their place and stole what few valuables they had.) Here I mention the younger couples, the ones who recently became homeowners and lost their houses to the floods that followed Katrina. But there are other people we know and their families, those who lived in Lakeview, in Mid-City, in Gentilly, in the Ninth Ward, in New Orleans East — all devastated neighborhoods — for years before having everything they own disintegrate in the dirty flood water.

We are fortunate to rent Uptown, where wind had caused damage. One oak limb landed on our second car and one landed in the back yard, thankfully not on the apartment's roof.

REMARKABLY, KIM'S TOILET STILL FLUSHES and the sink still coughs out water. Though there's no door on the bathroom, we have walls at this point in the demolition, and while others take a break outside, I go inside to relieve myself. The toilet is a muddy shade of light brown, the white porcelain having absorbed the muck from the flood. The bathtub is similarly muddy in color. Two broken blackened cubes of soap are stuck to the tiled-in soap dish just above the tub. They sit as if undisturbed, but their position gives an indication of how the water rose in Gentilly. It came up inch by inch, foot by foot, no sudden gush or tidal wave as in areas close to the failed levees. This house was dry until Tuesday after the storm.

Outside, we enjoy the mild December weather. We drink water and share po'boys. We know there's beer for the day's end. I finally talk with a young woman named Jennifer who has traveled from Virginia to help with the gutting. She's a low residency graduate student, and she came to New Orleans because she wanted to assist in some specific way. The spirit of volunteerism overwhelms me at times. Elsewhere in the city, teams of youth work in packs to distribute food and water, and groups of citizens gather weekly to pick up trash. It amazes me how many people are like this, willing to sacrifice their time for the city's recovery.

AFTER LUNCH, I TAKE A sledgehammer to the Sheetrock. When ripping apart Sheetrock, I learn, it's best to pull off large chunks. I learn as I do, using the sledge to make the initial dent and then peeling away the rest. Corners are tough, frustrating tasks, and the parts of the walls secured with chicken wire make me want to scream.

"You cocksucking motherfucker." It's Bill's partner and retained professor, Nancy, cursing at the reinforced Sheetrock. Not wanting to be mistaken for an academic, she speaks with a twang that lets everyone know she's spent most of her adult life in the south. Nancy chips away at a stubborn corner.

A large chunk of Sheetrock lands on my toes. Fortunately the sturdy boots I wear save me from serious injury. I learn to back off as larger pieces fall.

Soon the house pulses with the sound of destruction, a constant bam, bam, bam, bam, bam. As I smash one wall, someone hammers through the other side; bits of Sheetrock fly across the room. Jarret, who lost his instructor's job to cutbacks made since the storm and who's used his time since to create a post-Katrina online publication, crashes through the wall. He's lanky and moves awkwardly, like the prototypical white boy. A blue bandana covers his reddish beard and he wears mirrored sunglasses. He cocks the hammer back before sending it into the wall. The backswing is wasted motion, I want to tell him, but it's too loud to speak sensibly. I move to another wall in another room, one where I'll be away from flying Sheetrock.

"This is sort of a pleasure," Inge shouts, punching through the wall with a hammer. "I can really get into this."

I tear off a large piece of Sheetrock, finding satisfaction in ripping away a moldy two-foot slab.

We work for another few hours, pounding, ripping, and now tossing the junk on the curb. Around three-thirty we call it quits. The smokers seem to manage the physical exertion as well as the nonsmokers. Outside, we talk as we finish a twelve pack. We joke about the term deconstruction. We are dirty, tired, and by now, a little drunk.

At home my husband and I leave our filthy boots at the door, not wanting our cats to rub their faces against the potentially toxic dust that covers the footwear. Inside, after depositing our dirty clothes in the washer, we shower and then promptly pass out on the bed, naked, and too tired to think about dinner just yet. When we wake around seven, we have tired, lazy sex, both of us vying for the bottom, both of us surprised we still have it in us. This is how laborers get it done, I suppose.

WEDNESDAY IS ASBESTOS DAY. My husband and I arrive in the late morning to see that most of the ceiling has been knocked in by those who got here early, and with the ceiling went the fiberglass insulation. The floor of each room is buried in about two feet of the fluffy, itchy stuff as well as piles of Sheetrock and wood, nails, some glass, and junk, lots of junk from inside the ceiling and walls. Outside, the debris pile extends beyond the house and across the street to the neutral ground where someone has discarded a rusty lawnmower, an archaic stationary bicycle, and an R2D2 karaoke machine, useless things that should have been thrown away years ago.

I fill a wheelbarrow with the house's debris, haul it outside, dump it on the neutral ground, and return. The trickiest part involves the makeshift ramp that rests over the front steps. I find it's best to straddle the ramp and move backwards with the full wheelbarrow. Others still work to pull apart the house. They pry nails from the studs, chip away at stubborn Sheetrock, and smash in closet walls, while I clean up the junk. It's an endless task, one that only Sisyphus can appreciate. All the Sheetrock I tore down yesterday has got to be thrown away. And there's more, always more to be done. It's like the pile never stops growing. It never goes away.

Soon, I am itchy. Every bit of exposed skin tingles — my arms, my neck, my ears and the tiny parts of my face that are uncovered.

Nancy sees me scratching and says, "It's the fiberglass. Better rinse off with the hose, and put on a long-sleeved shirt."

I do as instructed and it helps, but now my nose won't stop running. Frequently after a wheelbarrow trip, I blow my nose. When I run out of tissue, I use the corner of my shirt.

During one of my trips outside, I feel my eyes burn. Rather, it's more of a stabbing sensation, like tiny knives slicing into my pupils. I say something about it and hear, "I had a meltdown yesterday with the same thing." It's Rachel, who arrives with po'boys. Yesterday she helped to gut the house, but today, after her eye-stabbing meltdown, she volunteers to keep us supplied with food and drinks.

"Must be fiberglass," Nancy offers. "Best thing to do is let your eyes tear up."

I try not rub or rinse my eyes. Instead I summon natural moisture, and the stabbing subsides, mutates into a dull headache.

AN IDAHO NATIVE OF HEARTY farmers' stock, Kim's a big woman. Her face is round, and from the nose up it reminds me of Hemingway's visage — high cheekbones, deep set eyes, and a wide forehead. Somewhere in her forties, Kim's exact age is difficult to discern. She has hay colored hair, gray eyes, and the kind of smooth skin my grandmother had, uncorrupted by makeup.

Ever since I've known her, Kim's been a jovial drunk, generous with hugs and kisses, full of mirth and laughter. When we break for lunch, Kim pulls out a bandana to wipe away tears. Since the storm, she cries often. Who wouldn't? There is no hiding the depression that has consumed her. Drinking doesn't help, and we all drink too much, this group of academics, and some of us smoke, Kim included. Now is not the time to quit.

Outside as we rest on coolers, we discuss what we took with us when we left the city four months ago. It's a common topic for conversation. "I took papers to grade," Inge laughs at her evacuation plans.

"Fuck that," Jarret says.

"I left mine in the office, hoping they'd be washed away," I offer.

One of the many great things about living down here in New Orleans is never knowing when it's going to end, when the slate will be wiped clean. Life can be a happy experience if we try to live like that, as if the end is near.

WHEN THE RED CROSS AMBULANCE passes through the neighborhood, we take what they offer — water and snacks. With the hard work our appetites are big. Another truck drives past the house; this one offers blankets, masks, and goggles that fog easily. A volunteer asks how we're doing and we say, "Fine."

"No, how are you really doing?" he repeats.

"We're doing okay," Nancy offers. "But our friend, the one whose house this is, she's not doing too good."

"We could send somebody by," he offers.

"That'd be nice."

Most houses in Kim's neighborhood sit quietly as if abandoned, and all are marked with spray painted orange X's, testaments to the search and rescue efforts made after the storm. Walking up to their windows, I can see which ones have been gutted, which ones have been emptied of their furniture, and which ones remain just as they did before the flood — full of furniture, full of stuff. Perhaps their owners came months ago, took what they could salvage, and left. At the house next door a once waterlogged car sits in the driveway, its chalky exterior further proof of destruction. Being just days after Christmas may explain why the block is so empty. It's fortunate, I guess, that other homeowners are not also gutting today since I cannot fathom where all this debris will go. Insulation and Sheetrock from Kim's house alone crowd her front yard, and the narrow neutral ground overflows with junk. Two blocks away in someone's front yard sits a FEMA trailer; it's uninhabited since no utilities except water are yet available here.

I walk over to the Saint James Playspot and note the water line on the sign. It's well above my head.

Over lunch, we discuss what Kim plans to do after the gutting. To date, she's undecided. Much depends on her neighbors and whether or not they come back. If no one returns, there won't be any neighborhood. She could raise the house six feet and rebuild it or sell it as is — gutted to the studs. When I hear that bulldozing is still an option, I get a little edgy — all this hard work and someone better live in this place.

After lunch, I set out to finish clearing one room of debris. Having a goal in mind will make the task easier. The front rooms are more or less clear, so I choose a room in the center of the house, the master bedroom. I devise a system. The hallway is too narrow and cramped for the wheelbarrow, so I push it up to the bare studs of the room. From there, I shovel piles of debris, passing them between the studs and into the wheelbarrow. Often the shovel catches on a nail, interrupting my flow, but I fight with the floor, wiggle the shovel, and manage to scoop some debris into the wheelbarrow. I squat and gather the small piles of rubble with my hands. Dust kicks up and makes me cough, makes my nose run.

Elsewhere in the house, my husband destroys the bathroom walls. From the corner of my eye I see what he's about to do and suggest removing the mirrored cabinet before smashing the wall, not so much to avoid the bad luck that supposedly comes with breaking a mirror but to avoid the dangerous mess of broken glass it will cause. But the poet in charge assures us it doesn't matter what we do — we've been walking on broken glass, nails, and debris for two days now, and besides, the whole thing has to go anyway, so the decision is made to just smash it.

MY HUSBAND AND I ARE in our thirties, and before Katrina hit, we considered becoming property owners. Our families fully reinforced this notion.

"Buy a house," was all we heard last year when we visited them in Rhode Island.

"It doesn't matter if you like it. You can get rid of it in six months. Just buy a house," my brother once said.

"We'd have to live in it," I pointed out.

Besides, we figured our rent and monthly expenses to be much less than the cost of a mortgage, and the debt we've acquired from graduate school and international excursions was also something to factor in. At the time, paying off the debt and waiting for the real estate market's bubble to burst seemed a more reasonable plan than investing in property. Well below the national average, our salaries are no help either. Our friends who work in education in other parts of the country guffaw when they hear what we make a year. (Now it must be even funnier since twenty percent of my salary's been cut since the storm.) Like most people in our line of work, we live paycheck to paycheck, but this is our choice. In the time-money equation, we always choose time.

"Just because it's possible doesn't mean it's a good idea." I am reminded of the Buddhist saying when I think about owning property or having children. It's possible; it always has been, but is it a good idea?

Kids cost money, and besides, we're selfish youngest children, unwilling to give up the way we live. We're not clothes hounds or electronics freaks, but we have our vices. We are unwilling to give up the wine we drink with dinner, the fresh ingredients we purchase for our meals, the first editions we read, and the cable television we need for viewing Friday Night Fights and Red Sox baseball. More importantly, we're unwilling to take jobs that would require more of our time than teaching does. If we save enough each paycheck, we can manage a summer without teaching, a summer free to write, play cards, read books, and take a few short trips.

I had less than two hundred dollars in my checking account when we left New Orleans for Katrina. If it weren't for my husband's online poker playing, we would have had to subsist on credit alone.

When the levees failed and eighty percent of the city flooded, I admit, I couldn't wait to remind our families of our complacency masked as foresight. I couldn't wait to say, "Aren't you glad we didn't buy a house? Aren't you glad we don't have a child to worry about?"

TIRED AND SORE, WE ARRIVE for our third day of gutting. The room I cleared yesterday is full with debris once again.

Where is this stuff coming from? The ceiling? The closets? Other rooms? I'm angry, angry that I worked so hard and have nothing to show for it. But what can I do now? I slide the mask over my face, put on my gloves, and haul more debris. Soon my nose is running again and I have to spit. I spend an hour or two clearing more junk from the room I just cleaned yesterday.

The wheelbarrow is too wide to reach the back rooms, and in those areas, I bend, scoop, and deposit piles of junk into a rubber trash barrel. Once it fills, I drag it out back where Carl, a white-haired English instructor, thumps it down the steps, attaches it to a dolly, and drags it across the street to the neutral ground. He works tirelessly. Today is Carl's first day on the job. We do this for hours, and later on, as Carl walks through one of the back rooms, a board falls on his head. He's stunned but thankfully not concussed.

Finally, the place is more or less clear. Kim and her contractor friend will come tomorrow to pry more nails and sweep. Then she'll wait to hear about her Small Business Association loan. Since the insurance money has dried up, everyone in the city with property in need of major repair waits for small business loans. In the meantime, Kim has applied for a FEMA trailer, one that will be housed on UNO's Lakefront campus. She's afraid she'll get too depressed if the trailer is put here, on her desolate block, and besides, at UNO she'll have lights, gas, and water.

AT HOME IN THE SHOWER, I taste something chalky — Sheetrock dust and fiberglass. It's dry, and I cough — now I've got it too, the Katrina cough. After the shower, I wash the chalky taste away with a beer and settle on the couch to read for a while but fall asleep instead. A nap at seven o'clock will keep me up late.

At night we head to the Goldmine, a French Quarter bar where Bill reads as part of a regular Thursday night venue. His political rants offer a well needed balance to the narcissistic poets who proceed and follow him. At the Goldmine we run into familiar faces now free of the masks, clean from dust. There, too, we run into one of my husband's colleagues and his wife whose name I never remember. I perfunctorily ask how they have been since Katrina. Once our Uptown neighbors, they run in similar circles as we do, and yet we manage to cross paths infrequently. When they tell me they're staying on the North Shore because the house they recently bought in Mid-City took on two feet of water, I tell them I'm sorry, though I'm not sure I truly am. He's a threat to my husband's job as both of them work toward retention, and I don't recall his wife ever smiling, even before the storm. Funny how those feelings never go away. When we talk about those who will come back to the city, it's not the ghetto's return I worry about.

BY THE TIME MARDI GRAS rolls around, Kim's trailer is still not ready, so she's made up her mind to rent a basement apartment in Mid-City, a place that took on water but is now almost fully repaired. It's the bottom part of a friend's place, and Kim seems comfortable and relieved to have somewhere to live, even if she doesn't own it. By the time her FEMA trailer arrives, the semester will be over; hurricane season will return. We recover from Fat Tuesday's festivities — yes, we celebrated with our usual stupidity. My husband has developed a deep, soul-jarring cough that wakes me in the night. Two days after Mardi Gras, in the midst of one of his many coughing fits, I answer the phone to find out that our apartment is being turned over to Latter and Blum, a realtor we jokingly refer to as "Latter and Doom." The rent will be raised, and we'll be locked into a lease. It's finally time, we decide, for us to buy a house.

We move quickly, knowing that places in good shape go fast. We can rip away Sheetrock, but we're not handy people capable of renovating a gutted home, we tell every real-estate agent who tries to sell us one. No, we cannot start from scratch. In a neighborhood known as the Bywater, officially the Ninth Ward, three blocks from the Industrial Canal — the side that didn't break this time — we find a lovely single shotgun. It's tiny, much smaller than our Uptown abode. Formerly a love nest for two queens, the cottage is in excellent condition — new electric, new plumbing, shiny hardwood floors, a slate roof and a bidet in the one bathroom. Yes, water did rush in with the storm surge, but it rushed out just as quickly as it came. All the places on the block had the same thing happen, and remarkably, all, but the one next door, built on a slab, seem fine.

We ride by the place at night; street lights glow and gay house music, the kind heard on St. Ann and Bourbon, sounds from the double next door. The dirty smell of spring hangs in the air. The house is a block off St. Claude Avenue, a messy street where flooded cars and junked items still litter the neutral ground. It's quite a change from where we live now, the Isle of Denial, my husband's term for Uptown. But we're ready, we decide, to sacrifice some space for the little piece of the Bywater.

ON TUESDAY AFTER THE HURRICANE, hundreds of miles away from New Orleans, we realized our city would be uninhabitable for some time and headed north to our families where we lived for six weeks in rent-free limbo. While on the road, we sensed that leaving it all behind wasn't such a bad thing. There was nothing in our apartment of real value. We had only each other and our indoor cats. We don't own property; we're not invested. We have portable skills. We can write, teach, bartend, learn a new trade, and do any of these things anywhere. But after three days of house gutting, after the destruction, after several post-apocalyptic months, we cannot help but be invested. We are committed.

D

Let me give you a description of my new residence. I never knew what the beauty of an old Creole home was until now. I do not believe one could find anything more picturesque outside of Venice or Florence. For six months I had been trying to get a room in one of these curious buildings; but the rents seemed to me maliciously enormous. However, I at last obtained one for $3 per week. Yet it is on the third floor, rear building; — these old princes of the South built always double edifices, covering an enormous space of ground, with broad wings, courtyards, and slave quarters.

The building is on St. Louis Street, a street several hundred years old. I enter by a huge archway about a hundred feet long, — full of rolling echoes, and commencing to become verdant with a thin growth of bright moss. At the end, the archway opens into a court. There are a few graceful bananas here with their giant leaves splitting in ribbons in the summer sun, so that they look like young palms. Lord! How the carriages must have thundered under that archway and through the broad paved court in the old days. The stables are here still; but the blooded horses are gone, and the family carriage, with its French coat of arms, has disappeared. There is only a huge wagon left to crumble to pieces. A hoary dog sleeps like a stone sphinx at a corner of the broad stairway; and I fancy that in his still slumbers he might be dreaming of a Creole master who went out with Beauregard or Lee and never came back again. Wonder if the great greyhound is waiting for him.

The dog never notices me. I am not of this generation, and I creep quietly by lest I might disturb his dreams of the dead South. I go up the huge stairway. At every landing a vista of broad archways reëchoes my steps — archways that once led to rooms worthy of a prince. But the rooms are now cold and cheerless and vast with emptiness. Tinted in pale green or yellow, with a ceiling moulded with Renaissance figures in plaster, the ghost of luxury and wealth seems trying to linger in them. I pass them by, and taking my way through an archway on the right, find myself on a broad piazza, at the end of which is my room.

It is vast enough for a Carnival ball. Five windows and glass doors open flush with the floor and rise to the ceilings. They open on two sides upon the piazza, whence I have a far view of tropical gardens and masses of building, half-ruined but still magnificent. The walls are tinted pale orange colour; green curtains drape the doors and windows; and the mantelpiece, surmounted by a long oval mirror of Venetian pattern, is of white marble veined like the bosom of a Naiad. In the centre of the huge apartment rises a bed as massive as a fortress, with tremendous columns on carved mahogany supporting a curtained canopy at the height of sixteen feet. It seems to touch the ceiling, yet it does not. There is no carpet on the floor, no pictures on the wall, — a sense of something dead and lost fills the place with a gently melancholy; — the breezes play fantastically with the pallid curtains, and the breath of flowers ascends into the chamber from the verdant gardens below. Oh, the silence of this house, the perfume, and the romance of it. A beautiful young Frenchwoman appears once a day in my neighborhood to arrange the room; but she goes like a ghost and disappears too soon in the recesses of the awful house.

LAFCADIO HEARN
from a letter to H.E. Krehbiel
1877

The University of New Orleans, a state university on the south shore of Lake Pontchartrain, was a refuge for about two thousand storm victims for a week after Katrina made landfall on August 29, 2005. Some had fled to its high ground from flooded homes in the northern precincts of Gentilly, an integrated middle-class neighborhood. Some had been airlifted there. To get food and water, the refugees broke into campus stores. They slept in classrooms and lobbies. All the city's water and sewage pumps had failed, so the refugees relieved themselves where they could. They were the first to survey the adjacent wasteland of Gentilly, day and night.

Ghostland Sublime
KRIS LACKEY

On September 5, a vanguard of university administrators was "inserted" by military boats and troops to retrieve vital records. Not long after, energy crews erected utility poles and highlines to replace flooded underground lines. Later in the fall of 2005, UNO's administration returned and occupied the Education Building, a late-sixties' bunker with pillbox slits for windows, which alone remained completely functional after the storm. From that redoubt they salvaged a semester. And each day, they drove through miles of wasteland — tens of thousands of vacant homes pasted with grey mud, tens of thousands of ruined cars and trucks, tens of thousands of dead and wind-wracked oaks and pines and magnolias.

The autumn of 2005 is known at UNO as the Katrina Semester. Most faculty members were displaced by the storm, and most taught online. The school's six thousand registered students that semester, the majority of whom were far-flung, peered at computer screens, read assigned books, and typed essays in Boston, Portland, Lubbock, Memphis, Oklahoma City. By the spring semester of 2006, a majority of the faculty had returned, as had about 11,000 of UNO's pre-Katrina student population of 17,000.

The week before spring classes began in late January 2006, my colleagues in the English department drifted in to check their teaching schedules and survey their offices, which had been "mold-remediated." A few globs of antibiotic slime hung on desks and bookcases, a medicinal odor wafted through the ventilation ducts. A few of our personal effects — staplers, photographs, radios (but no books) — had been removed along with the mold.

Most of my colleagues had not seen one another since Friday, August 26, the last day of classes before Katrina. All we knew about those who were not our close friends we had read in an emailed department directory that furnished addresses, phone numbers, and brief narratives of our evacuation and post-K circumstances. "I am living with my brother and his family in Salt Lake City." "We have stayed with friends in four states and are currently in Asheville."

When we meet in the halls we are shy. Even abashed. Some UNO people were airlifted from submerged homes to refugee camps, and others drove away and later returned to dry and functioning houses and apartments. Exactly who had suffered what we do not yet know, and we are tentative. We embrace, regardless of sex, and the hugs are long and tight. Everyone has traversed the wasteland on the way to campus, and everyone has been weeping. A male colleague confesses that he has seldom cried in his adult life but drives to work every day through a blur of tears.

Exile has left its mark on our bodies and faces, as if the varied forms of ruin visited on the city's homes trailed us and possessed us. Half of us have swollen like soaked rafters. Half of us have withered like tide-poisoned boxwood. Moldy walls are stained teeth, wind-frayed curtains our shaggy hair. Some of us have aged a hundred years, like our Van Winkle houses. Some of us have spooked-stallion eyes. We are a mess. Our outfits come from Wal-Mart and the Sally Army. And we, most of us, are the lucky ones.

The semester begins. A few professors conduct class in scalloped white wedding tents. The power often fails. There are no elevators. The only food service is lodged in a distant building. Some classrooms smell of urine. Teachers, staff and students shamble across campus, dour or comically distrait.

Still and all, the University of New Orleans campus qualifies as one of the city's "isles of denial" — places where trees and grass survive, there is no debris, and the architecture is more or less intact. Places where you can look all around and see nothing grossly out of the ordinary. This mental calculus transforms a gaggle of bottom-line Soviet buildings into a *hortus conclusus*, an enclosed garden, as Solomon and the old Latin poets would have it. But first, you have to get there.

No one comes from New Orleans East. Everything from campus ten miles east to the Chef Menteur Pass lies silent. Those who come from the high, intact settlements of Bywater, the Quarter, the Marigny, Uptown, and the Esplanade Ridge cross into the ghostland when they descend I-10 overpasses on Wisner or Elysian Fields into Gentilly. Then they drive four miles through untenanted cottages and modest Tudor houses and ranch homes before they reach the Isle. Those who come from Jefferson Parish, to the west, cross into the wasteland on Old Hammond Highway, over the 17th Street Canal very near the infamous breach. Before they gain the Isle, they must traverse four miles of ruined Lakeview, once a prosperous and largely white precinct of the city. Every student, staff member, and professor who arrives at the University of New Orleans each day sees what disaster tourists from around the world pay to gawk at through a bus window. But the tourists will fly away. They will go home. And we are, more or less, home.

The ravaged basins we cross assault the eye. Subdivisions built from the forties onward aped fashion alien to the city, from faux Tudor to ranch to modern eclectic. They were ugly when they were built, but decades of tropical heat and moisture smudged their crude pragmatic angles with massive oaks, lush banana trees, husky magnolias, and tentacular jasmine. Most residents landscaped their yards with day lilies and azalea and lantana and camellias. They fertilized and manicured thick lawns of St. Augustine grass. Katrina's surge put the basins under eight feet of seawater for weeks. Retreating water left a sepia ghostworld.

Stark mud-caked brick facades, bearing the National Guard's fluorescent calculus — 1 D, 0 L, rise from brittle nests of gray shrubs and grass. The stripped boles and limbs of water oaks and loblolly pines cant perilously, dripping trains of gray vines. Mounds of household debris — mold-stained mattresses and drapes, tide-wracked chairs and nasty dolls — line the curbs. Abandoned dogs slalom around the debris, circling their lost homes. Emerson said that the eye is the best of artists, but here, for miles, the eye jukes from street to horizon to house, unappeased. Not an inch of the earth affords the slightest aesthetic relief.

But ugliness does not make us weep in our automobiles

and arrive at school spent and shaky. No, the ghosts do that. The ghosts lived in those houses. Not just the houses on our thoroughfares — Wisner, Robert E. Lee, Elysian Fields — but the houses behind those and the houses behind those.

All who witnessed the aftermath on television know that the poor suffered much more than the relatively solvent citizens of inundated Gentilly. A third of New Orleanians did not own automobiles, and there was no plan to evacuate them. Fourteen hundred citizens, many of them very young or very old, perished in the floods. Beloved pets were executed by families about to be winched from rooftops and overpasses. Tens of thousands of impoverished survivors whose families had lived in New Orleans for centuries were airlifted or bused away, never to return. In the distant Lower Ninth, the revenants are multiplied almost to infinity, like Immanuel Kant's mathematical sublime. The pi of ghostland.

Some real ghosts haunt the Gentilly ghostland, like the three elderly people within a block of my Legion Oaks house who refused to evacuate and who drowned, and the two middle-aged men in the same neighborhood whose hearts failed in distant cities. Strangely, unless we lost loved ones the living ghosts trouble us more deeply. Their silent ruined homes speak to us as we drive past, each blurting half a frantic sentence before the next begins, a Babel of voices mounting and swirling into mad chatter, subsiding as we leave them behind.

We cannot, even as literature professors trained to respect honest realism and to ridicule sentimentality, make the ghosts choose between them. In the debris we see photograph albums, big wheelers, swing sets, cribs. But we also see bench saws, sewing machines, toolboxes, computer keyboards, broken dishes, and lawnmowers. The landscape of futility doesn't discriminate.

The revenants tell us what their evicted bodies will not, if they want to go about the business of living. Refugees say "These are only things. We have our lives." If we believed this truism, we could, as we traverse the ghostland, buck up against the mess, raise the volume on some ragtime from WWOZ, and think of the future. But the revenants say there is a death in life, too.

Residents of close-in suburbs like Gentilly and New Orleans East and my own Legion Oaks on the lakefront share with more distant suburbanites a dedication to house and garden, the tiny Estate. Middle-aged and elderly residents spend their evenings and weekends and much of their income keeping pace with — or, if they are wealthy enough — outstripping, the death-in-life march of the elements. New Orleans receives on average about fifty inches of rain a year. Some years see a hundred — eight feet of rain. For four months the high temperature sits around ninety degrees, broiling housepaint and shingles and rotting damp wood. Each spring, millions of Formosan termites hatch from rotted tree boles and form new colonies in damp attics and soffits. Each year, the suburban topsoil, unreplenished by Mississippi floods, sinks palpably.

Homeowners fight the battle on two flanks. On one, they combat the elements. To beat subsidence, they haul in truckloads of Mississippi River sand from the Bonnet Carré spillway and spread it on their yards. They shore their tipping houses, replacing rotted piers — which were sunk thirty feet through muck into sturdy, ancient beach sand — with new wooden piers or stacks of concrete cylinders. They replace rotting soffits and screens. And they paint. A lot.

On the other flank they combat wood-devouring insects — carpenter ants, subterranean termites, and, most militantly, Formosan termites. The last, an exotic species borne to the city on freighters from Asia, swarm on late spring evenings, billowing from the earth-line of infested trees like spectral cyclones. They dodge conventional termiticide barriers and nest in walls and attics, often devouring large sections of frame before they are detected. Before new buried-bait systems came into general use, it was common to see houses tented for fumigation. As the carnivalesque tents were folded, carpenters waited in the wings to replace gnawed studs, flooring, and wallboard.

The revenants have abandoned rusted tillers, reciprocating saws, hoes, ratchets, and nail guns. These tokens of futility sometimes crown the piles of debris because their handlers cherished their transforming agency and were loath to relinquish them. Such tools serve a different purpose from faucet wrenches, hammers, and paint rollers—the instruments of maintenance. Maintaining one's house in a fierce subtropical climate comes first, but that is like breathing. Through a straw. Creating gardens, remodeling kitchens, and designing additions — these endeavors dance. They fuel the daydreams of middle-class women and men at their jobs, inspire them to rise from their dinners and make a lasting mark on their small milieux.

My friends Howard Darlington and Carol Antosiac twist among the revenants. They lived with their daughter Quinn, my daughter's good friend, a block from where I did, in a square, raised brick two-bedroom ranch house, which I pass on the way to and from work. Carol managed an independent book store, and Howard was a self-employed foreign car mechanic. For fifteen years before the flood, they dragged home from long days, made dinner, and returned to work, transforming a squat plain ranchie into a garden home.

Carol sculpted landscape fore and aft, planting jasmine, heritage roses, ginger, lime trees, shrimp flowers, and herbs.

She dug a pond in the backyard, stocked it with golden carp, and erected an Asian portal. She repainted the interior of the house and, because she and Howard earned a modest living, furnished it and dressed the windows a little each season.

Howard tore out the sclerotic galvanized plumbing and replaced it with pvc. He refurbished the bathroom and tiled the kitchen. He designed and built a lovely high-gabled outbuilding, which he finished and plumbed for a laundry room. When he had spare spare time, he rebuilt and customized a yellow 1968 Sunbeam convertible, which he drove to rallies across the South.

When the London Avenue Canal's flimsy seawalls were breached on both sides, Katrina's storm surge inundated Carol and Howard's home from the western break. In a matter of hours, the decades of work they had spent on their home vanished. Six feet of seawater churned in their bedrooms and kitchen and living room for two weeks. The meticulously restored Sunbeam rusted solid.

Both of our daughters had returned to distant colleges just before the storm. They watched on television as the landmarks of their childhood sank like Atlantis. They angrily muted the rants of dolts and fools who blamed them and their families for what they had lost.

Two years later, most of their neighborhood had been hauled to landfills. They would never revisit their homes, Ferrara's grocery, the Gentilly post office, their elementary school, or the PJ's coffee shop where they met high school friends to study. Their parents had moved away — my wife and I to a rented Victorian shotgun double in the high ground of Mid-City, Carol and Howard to a *fin de siecle* cottage in Abbeville. By the fall of 2007, Legion Oaks' oaks were no longer legion. Most of the live oaks survived, stripped of small limbs and bristling along the spines with tiny new

branches, but the more common water oaks and laurel oaks
— fast-growing swamp trees — had fallen or snapped or
been poisoned by salt water. Legion Oaks has become a rural
space — a few ruined houses, some faux Creole or Victorian
modulars jacked high on cinderblock, and acres of emptiness.

Less than a year after the storm, my daughter came home
from a summer job. Before that, my wife and I had been
visiting her at college from our outposts. One afternoon
we drove toward Lake Pontchartrain from Mid-City along
Bayou St. John, passing three of City Park's golf courses,
now crazy with weeds and guarded by looming corpse trees.
When we crossed the bayou into our old neighborhood, the
first ghost houses appeared, bearing the fatal spray-painted
Guard codes. Susan began biting her nails. As we turned onto
Burbank Drive, she burst into tears.

Piles of debris from gutted houses lined the street. Most
of the houses were windowless, their trim blackened by
mold. All vegetation, save the stripped live oaks and a weird
multitude of sunflowers sprung from birdseed, was dead.
Once a shady street, canopied by forty-foot water oaks and
laurel oaks and cypress, it now baked in a midsummer glare,
its homes and their curbside bowels luridly exposed. Not a
single car or human figure appeared.

Susan wept for the same reason all of us who had returned
before her had mourned. A great natural force snuffed human
works and days, pushing close to us, on a vast scale, the grim
lesson of Ecclesiastes: Vanity of vanities, saith the Preacher,
vanity of vanities; all is vanity. What profit hath a man of all
his labour which he taketh under the sun?

New Orleanians — those who fled and never returned,
those who took their own lives, those who drowned, those
who came back and rebuilt, those who perished from grief,
those who lost their marriages, those who went mad — all of

them heard the Preacher. Even the boosters and pioneers and children heard him. His voice does not balk the survivors' work, in New Orleans or in Chicago or Atlanta, but he shadows their pursuits. They hear his whispered truth: they know that their labor under the sun is nonce work.

It never seemed to go away. The mold. The poison sadness of mold. The shock of it burned the nose, sharp prickly toxicity, like cocaine cut with something foul, sucked into her head where it could pull memories of that first autumn from her brain stem. Debris, rotting refrigerators. Buzzing of the crypt flies harmonizing with the buzzing dizziness in her head, the dust clouds sticking to the permanent lump in her throat.

Gather the Fragments that Remain

a short story by RAY SHEA

The flies and refrigerators were long gone now, more than three years later, but as she unlocked the front door for possibly the last time, she could feel her throat constricting once again.

The dust and grit of remodeling attempts long-since-abandoned powdered every surface. Newly installed framing glowed in the corner next to the older studs, where the flood-soaked Sheetrock had given way to reveal termite colonies almost as old as she was. Between the two-by-fours, old and new, brand new wiring ran to shiny new switch boxes, or stopped at dead-ends capped off by the last "electrician" (the third? fourth? she couldn't remember) to take a crack at the job, take a chunk of the money and then disappear. The Sheetrock delivery from a year ago lay stacked in the middle of the room, untouched, patiently waiting its turn, its usefulness rendered moot by an electrical inspection that had never come, that now would likely never come.

In any other gutted house — and she had gutted her share — she would have just stepped between the posts to go from room to room, but muscle memory took her down familiar paths, obeying the architecture as if the walls were more than suggestions, down the hall, to her old bedroom. The overgrowth in the side alley outside blocked the late-morning sun from penetrating the small window, and she reached for the light switch, reflex built over a lifetime, passing her hand over the wall by the door, finding a grimy, cracked toggle which she flicked up and down a few times, not comprehending at first why it failed to light the dimness.

The switch had somehow been spared the ravages of the swarm of crowbar-wielding volunteers who had "helped" her gut her childhood home in those first few months. Dreadlocked locusts from elsewhere, with righteous anger in their hearts, they stripped the house of everything non-structural with the energy and unsentimental detachment of youth. Everything except this one light switch, with its plastic Mickey Mouse switch cover she'd bought at Disney World, on the trip they took in her twelfth summer, after her father died. The mouse was barely discernable in bas relief in the dim light, the image stripped ivory white by time, by the palm sweat of a lifetime of grubby hands switching on and off, and finally by the flood water itself.

She traced a finger over the plastic, remembering how far it seemed from here to her bed, when at bedtime she had to shut off the light and run back in the dark, jumping from far enough out that whatever it was that lived under her bed couldn't possibly reach out far enough to grab her ankle. She recalled the one time she misjudged, miscounted steps and the top of her foot connected with the sharp underside of the corner of the bed frame. She still carried a crescent-moon scar where the metal had gouged a flap of skin, the scar faded over time, like the plastic Mickey, unrecognizable unless you knew what you were looking for and where to look for it.

In the back bedroom, her mother's bedroom, just a few boxes remained, stacked in the center of the floor waiting to be loaded into the van. The only possessions that had not been taken apart and consumed by the flood or hauled to the curb in a wheelbarrow and dumped like garbage filled a mere half dozen U-Stor-It boxes. Her parents' wedding china. Some pictures that had been salvaged from the highest closet shelves. The brass crucifix that always hung on the wall between the bedroom windows that looked out into the backyard.

She used to sit for hours at those windows, in the fall when she wasn't yet old enough to go to school with the neighborhood kids, warm quiet September mornings with her father at work, her mother in the kitchen ironing or cleaning up after breakfast. She'd kneel on the window seat, elbows on the sill, and keep watch over the sunflower that her mother had planted for her outside, the flower she'd grown from a seedling in day care that summer. Every day a bumblebee would visit, would hover and crawl and buzz around the flower. She could hear the deep thrumming through the glass, and it made her heart race a little to be so close to something as scary as a giant stinging bee.

The yard was overgrown now, almost chest high in places. For a while after the house had been gutted, she'd managed to keep it trimmed back, but as the remodel dragged on and then stalled, the effort seemed more and more futile. The drive across town from her tiny temporary rental in the Lower Garden District to the land of the flood was rarely worth the effort any more. These days the swamp was reclaiming vast stretches of what once was a "family" neighborhood, turning long-settled land back into delta thicket.

Far across the suburban jungle she could see her father's lemon tree, near the back fence, bearing fruit which was now made inaccessible by the encroaching wilderness.

A drop of sweat fell from the end of her nose, splashing a clean spot in the dust on the sill. Jesus, it was hot. She wiped her face on her sleeve, then hefted a box and walked it through the house and out to the van.

A bicycle approached, casually navigated by an ageless black man. Not old but truly ageless, age-indeterminate. Weathered by the passage of time or the toughness of a life of hard work or poverty, or all of these, it was hard to say. A trucker cap shielded his eyes from the June sun. His wiry, muscled arms stood out in stark relief through the cut-off sleeves of his white t-shirt.

A glance and a quick smile, a flash of gold.

"All right."

It seemed to her the customary greeting of the ageless black man, the answer pre-empting the unasked-but-assumed "How you doin'?" The "all right" was now routinely offered as call rather than response in that peculiar way that New Orleans has with weirding language.

She nodded "hey" and shoved the box into the back of the minivan, one eye watching as he passed by and continued on down the street, river bound. She turned toward the house, paused, turned back and closed the van hatch, considered locking it, wondering if he would interpret the beep of the keyless lock as an accusation. The daily internal conflict, trust versus fear, wariness of strangers shot through with a healthy dose of white guilt.

It took fifteen minutes to load the rest of the boxes, the

gravitational pull of mid-summer making each box heavier than the last even as the work should have gone more quickly as she decided that closing and reopening the hatch on every trip was tiresome and unnecessary. She had to move a toolbox aside to slot the last box in, but it went in with room to spare. The remains of an entire lifetime lived in one house fit easily, pitifully so, in the back of a minivan.

She pulled a bottle of water from her small ice chest and took it up to the porch to cool off and rest and catch a bit of the remaining shade as the sun approached merciless noon. The cold drink went down with an icy sharpness, almost painful. A sliver of ice slid down the side of the plastic, hanging off the bottom of the bottle briefly before letting go and falling onto the concrete steps where it boiled away instantly into nothing.

The sky was a stark and soulless blue, the nothing-blue like that of the Midwest skies she'd learned to hate in her decades since college. She'd spent those years running from this city, from her family, from her past, from her grief, distracting herself by chasing a career two thousand miles to the north, until Katrina dragged her back home and gave her a purpose. A house to restore, a city to rebuild, a childhood to reclaim.

"Creepy sun," she muttered. That had been a running joke with her friends all through college. They'd stumble uncertainly out of Miss Mae's or Andy Capp's at eight in the morning, wondering where the night went, blearily blinking into the creepy sun and looking for car keys.

There would be no afternoon thunderstorm to take the edge off this day, no brief respite of interesting weather to push back the heavy damp blanket and let a person breathe. Not even a passing fluffy cloud off the Gulf would run interference against the creepy sun today.

She squinted down the deserted street. Most of the families she'd grown up with had left years ago for the promised land of Jefferson Parish or the North Shore. The Sayers, the Heberts, the Kaufmans. Back then nobody had fences and the summer evening games of Kick the Can ranged through every yard, back and front. Every yard except for old Mr. Moreau's, down at the corner, whose entire front yard had been enclosed by hedges and God help any kid who had to go chase a ball in there.

And across the street had lived the Giarellis with their four boys. Mister Giarelli (Mister Tony to the neighborhood kids) used to get a kick out of tormenting old man Moreau every New Year's Eve with his giant fireworks party, shooting bottle rockets over his house and sending screeching red and blue spinners up his driveway, Moreau powerless to do anything about it since a call to the police would just bring Mister Tony's cousin the cop around to make sure everybody was having a good time. The Giarelli boys used to call those spinners "nigger chasers," which always made her squirm a little; even at a young age the casual bigotry of this city felt instinctively wrong to her.

The Moreau hedges were gone, along with the house. Just an empty overgrown lot with a "For Sale By Owner" sign leaning crookedly against a discarded water heater. And across the street, the late Mister Tony's house was all fixed up and occupied, but she didn't really know the people who lived there. Black folks. They seemed nice enough, although, like a lot of the neighbors who had moved here in the last decade or so before Katrina, they'd fenced in the front yard and hung a "BEWARE OF DOG" sign on the front gate.

She didn't imagine the neighborhood kids played much Kick The Can any more, not that there were any neighborhood kids left since the storm.

The rest of the houses on the block stood empty, gutted

and boarded, or gutted and abandoned and overgrown. Families gone with no regrets, or no means to return. Homes no longer homes. A city no longer recognizable. The childhood she had spent so many years running from, too many years to even account for, as if they had not passed one at a time but had scuttled by in twos and threes while her back was turned, the childhood that was no longer hers to return to, spirited away and supplanted by a homunculus of mold, weeds, neglect and corruption.

She stood up and tossed her empty water bottle into the weeds by the porch. She fished the house keys out of her pocket, the spare set that always used to hang on a hook in the kitchen next to the fridge, attached to a vintage plastic key tag advertising Harry's Ace Hardware. As she pulled the door closed, it stuck a little on the bottom jamb, like it always did in summer, the wood swelling and shrinking with the humidity as reliably as any weatherman's sensor, and she had to yank it hard to shut it. She twisted the key in the bolt lock and felt it click into place for the last time.

The lawyer handling the estate sale wanted the keys dropped off at his office, but she planned on calling him from the road on Monday to tell him where he could find them. One more day of despair in this city was one more day she had no intention of facing. She lifted the mailbox lid, its black aluminum hinges creaking in protest after almost four years of disuse. She dropped the keys inside, and gently shut it again.

Dusting her hands off on her shorts, she turned and walked slowly down the steps and across the lawn to the street, not wanting to look back. She sniffled and wiped her nose on her sleeve, wiped a tear and beeped the van open.

"You tryin' to get lost in New Orleans?"

It was the man on the bicycle again, heading back in the direction of the lake, carrying an impossibly long segment of galvanized steel gutter. He steered the bike with one hand, holding the gutter under the other arm, resting the length of it on the handlebars, pointing it out in front of him like an oversized rifle.

She stood with the driver's door open and tilted her head to the side, one foot on the street, one already in the car.

"Um … I'm not lost."

He flashed the smile again as he passed, close enough for her to see the two gold uppers, the bottoms gapped and disarmingly crooked.

"That's what I'm tryin' to do. Know what I'm sayin'?"

She watched him wobble away up the street. He put his foot down only once and she could hear him laugh at himself from down the block, then wobble back upright and almost jump the opposite curb before hitting his stride and pedaling off into the noon glare.

"I'm not lost," she repeated as she gazed down the empty street, watching him disappear into the ghost neighborhood.

She slumped down sideways on the driver's seat, her strength departing, her legs dangling out of the open door as she wiped tears from both cheeks. She squinted across the street at the Kaufman's house, with its overgrown yard and its spray-painted "X" on the brick façade next to the boarded-up front door. Then next door at the old Giarelli house, with its new windows, freshly laid sod and bright yellow flowers growing in a neatly mulched bed.

"I'm not lost."

The flowers were tall and very beautiful.

She sat up suddenly, dug around in the back seat until she found a screwdriver and trotted back up to the house.

A minute later she returned, ponytail bouncing, and hopped in the driver's seat, tossing the screwdriver into the back. She gently laid the Mickey Mouse switch plate next to her on the passenger seat, then twisted the key in the ignition and slowly pulled away from the curb, humming a little Fats Domino tune.

The plastic Harry's key tag dangled from the steering column, the house keys jingling in time to Fats and to the bouncing of the van as she navigated the potholed streets.

She put on her sunglasses and smiled.

And in the new flowerbed of the old Giarelli place, an ageless bumblebee lumbered from sunflower to sunflower, working patiently, methodically, gathering pollen, dropping pollen, the same as it had done yesterday, the same as it would do tomorrow.

"I don't care if I never see the
city again. Honestly, they treat
me better all over the world
than they do in my home town.
Ain't it stupid? Jazz was born
there, and I remember when it
wasn't no crime for cats of any
color to get together and blow."

LOUIS ARMSTRONG,
1949, after returning to New
Orleans to lead the Zulu parade
and facing the racism of a
Jim Crow city

"I don't know about y'all, but I'm sure damn tired of people asking me is New Orleans coming back. I'm so sick of that question. I tell 'em, *I* tell 'em all the time, Goddamn right we're coming back, 'cause we don't like y'all food and we hate y'all music. [cheers and applause] Right? Y'all know what's up. I came home, I had a fried oyster and like to cried. I said damn that's good! [laughing] Oooh, shit."

Terence Blanchard, April 29, 2006, at the New Orleans Jazz and Heritage Fest

PART TWO

Culture & History.

❷

"If you think that your culture is a leisure activity, it belies a level of deep and profound ignorance. That's why you will have trouble with your business practices, like we have trouble with our business practices in the United States, because we lack integrity. What informs your integrity is your culture, and your culture is your stories, your songs. That is your integrity, and when that is for sale and when everything is for sale, you lose your mooring. Where is home? You don't know where home is, and once you don't know where home is, you could be anywhere."

Ⓖ

Wynton Marsalis, May 4, 2009, on "The Life and Times of Irvin Mayfield," WGSO, 990 AM

It is not an easy thing to describe one's first impression of New Orleans; for while it actually resembles no other city upon the face of the earth, yet it recalls vague memories of a hundred cities. It owns suggestions of towns in Italy, and in Spain, of cities in England and in Germany, of seaports in the Mediterranean, and of seaports in the tropics. Canal street, with its grand breadth and imposing facades, gives one recollections of London and Oxford street and Regent street; there are memories of Havre and Marseilles to be obtained from the Old French Quarter; there are buildings in Jackson Square which remind one of Spanish-American travel. I fancy that the power of fascination which New Orleans exercises upon foreigners is due no less to this peculiar characteristic than to the tropical beauty of the city itself. Whencesoever the traveler may have come, he may find in the Crescent City some memory of his home — some recollection of his Fatherland — some remembrance of something he loves.

from LAFCADIO HEARN,
"At the Gate of the Tropics," *Cincinnati Commercial*,
November 19, 1877

1

I would like to tell the story of my city.

I would like to do so in simple, declarative sentences. I would like my narrative to be neat and linear, like I learned in school and on television. Do not think me unequal to the task. In fact, I have already started a draft:

Still Live, with Voices

LOLIS ERIC ELIE

"We were founded by the Europeans. They taught us to cook and to speak French and to look down on the Americans. We were built by the Africans. They had tremendous talent for dancing and singing and following European instruction. We were saved by the non-Native Americans. They taught us to work hard and to honor the dollar and to cherish the word freedom even more than the condition itself. Then the gods of misfortune stirred the winds of disaster and left us clinging Noah-like for dear life in the flooding of three years ago."

As you can see, my city has three parents, not counting the gods and the winds who have shaped us as surely as any DNA. I myself have two parents — a kind, sweet mother and a most unruly father. The neatness of every draft I compose is ruined by these five voices, voices that suddenly pop out like the wild hairs that have escaped the barber's scissors unclipped.

So we Africans, the Africans in you, are nothing more than dancing beasts with wild hair?

No one is anything yet, father. It is a draft and we are all in a state of becoming.

In a state of becoming sold down the river again.

Excuse me, Kemo Sabe, but when the Europeans were doing their founding, they founded us already here. Put that in your story. More voices, you must have more voices.

I will have more voices, I'm sure, invited or not.

2

"For much of the 19th century, New Orleans was the economic powerhouse of the southern United States. The city has spent millions to recapture that greatness. The investment may one day pay off. But, in the meantime, we are known principally for two things: our food and our music. They grow so naturally here as to be deemed by our city fathers as hardly worthy of investment.

"In the matter of food we were instructed by the French, whose reputation for culinary genius is time-tested and well earned. Subsequent Europeans — the Spanish, the Sicilians, the Germans — have all left their culinary mark. Black cooks, with their innate sense of seasoning, have also lent their peculiar je ne sais quoi to our culinary heritage."

Do not blame us for your food, monsieur. Your poisson meuniere is deep fried; your remoulade is red and has no anchovies; your "French" bread has a crust like phyllo dough, not like a proper baguette, and you put that slimy okra in your bouillabaisse. Your food is good, peut-etre. Peut-etre. But Francais? Jamais!

Okay, it's Creole. It's our version of French. It's France in

America plus 300 years plus black cooks.

Why do you insist on crediting the French with everything? That bouillabaisse is neither bouillabaisse nor French. It's okra soup. It's soupa konja. It's west African; just like jambalaya. And can you imagine Creole food without rice? We were growing rice in Senegal before the French knew how to plant it. And these vague "Africans" you refer to had countries — Senegal, Benin, Cameroun, etc. It's been documented.

Have either of you read the books about our food? They all say the same thing. Genius French chefs. Talented black cooks. Don't blame me.

I hate to darken your narrative again, Kemo Sabe, but the filé in your gumbo is the sassafras leaf powder we introduced to your people.

If I might please continue. . .

You might, but you will be the only one pleased.

3

"Opera has been performed in New Orleans since the 1700s and there were even celebrated free people of color playing and composing classical music. But our city is best known for jazz. That music has its roots in Congo Square, the area where black people, slave and free, played music and danced dances that linked back to Africa.

Not that "jazz comes from Africa" foolishness again!

I didn't say jazz came from Africa!

And you didn't say anything about American marching bands. What about all that European harmony and those European instruments? What about all those New Orleans trumpet players who learned from the Herbert L. Clarke and Arban method books? The whole of jazz is little more than theme and variations a la "Carnival of Venice." And if not for B.A. Rolfe's inspiration, would Louis Armstrong ever have soared into the upper register of his talents?

Yes, but all the greatest musicianers — Louis Armstrong, Jelly Roll Morton, Joe "King" Oliver — they were all black.

"In the 1950s, New Orleans emerged as a capital of rhythm and blues. New Orleans artists like Dave Bartholemew, Fats Domino and Lloyd Price topped the charts while stars like Little Richard recorded hits here. In the 1990s New Orleans topped the charts in popular music again as a result of the success of two record labels, No Limit and Cash Money."

I suppose there's no room for the white people in your so-called history.

White people were the architects of this city. Didn't I say that?

4

"Two streets exemplify the architectural heritage of New Orleans, Esplanade and St. Charles avenues. The former is the grand boulevard of the Creoles. The houses are close to the banquette and tend to hide the grandeur within. St. Charles Avenue, with its large front yards and front porches exemplifies the style of the American sector. Much of the construction was done by free people of color who all but dominated the building trades in the antebellum period."

Yes, but your Americans tried to put an end to that dominance. They declared it illegal to hire black craftsmen to work on public buildings.

That may be, but even now many of the top carpenters in town are black men with French surnames.

Señor, I have not troubled to disturb your little narration before, but the Spanish built the French Quarter. Most of what the French built was destroyed in the fires of 1788 and 1794. And these free people of color you keep referring to. Most of them were freed during the period of Spanish rule.

If all that's true, then why don't they call it the Spanish Quarter?

Now, señor, you're asking my question.

5

"The two New Orleans topics that have most consistently enthralled outsiders have been the topics of race or, to put it more precisely, miscegenation and corruption."

How is that two topics?

"Centuries of trans-racial liaisons have resulted in a large population of light brown Creoles who at times have been seen, and seen themselves, as a separate caste."

I have never heard of a black or brown Creole. The Creoles are white descendents of the original white Spanish and French settlers.

"Yet among the free people of color and their descendants were also scores of radical egalitarians. They produced the first African American daily newspaper, *La Tribune de la Nouvelle Orleans*, and actually sent a delegation who met with, and demanded voting rights from, President Lincoln. Their fight for equality culminated in the Plessy v. Ferguson Supreme Court case in which it was declared that "separate but equal" segregation was consistent with American democracy."

If these light skinned Creoles were so egalitarian why did they look down on dark skinned people? You remember what happened when ol' brown George Lewis and his black clarinet showed up to a gig at one of those Creole functions? The woman at the door asked the band leader, 'Where did you get that?' She wasn't talking about the clarinet.

6

"The city has earned a reputation for corruption, perhaps dating as far back as the colonial period when various schemes were used to convince settlers to move to Louisiana. Recent indictments of public officials have done little to reverse this perception."

That's that French legacy you people are so proud of. If we hadn't bought you, New Orleans would be an even bigger cesspool.

Vraiment? Well, mon ami, how do you explain this: the schemer who duped my people into investing in this mosquito-infested back water was John Law, a Scotsman.

My son, have you noticed that no one ever forgets the corruption in New Orleans, where the political leaders are black, and no one ever remembers the corruption in Alaska, Rhode Island, Texas and the halls of Congress, where most of the accused and convicted are white? Curious thing, memory.

7

"When Hurricane Katrina struck the Gulf Coast, and 80 percent of New Orleans was flooded, many Americans blamed the high water on the culture of corruption and the tolerance of sin that they say was emblematic of New Orleans."

Was there or was there not going to be a gay pride parade in New Orleans? I said it then and I'll say it now: my God will not sit idly by as heathen Sodomites mock His Holy Name.

"While thousands of New Orleanians were trapped in floodwaters and on roofs, President George Bush flew by the area in an airplane. A delegation of Canadian Mounties arrived in the New Orleans area a few days after the storm to provide assistance. Days later, the government of the United

States began to provide meaningful assistance to its citizens.

"More than two dozen countries offered assistance to the victims of Hurricane Katrina, but they found the American government less than enthusiastic about accepting aid. As Bush told ABC news, 'I'm not expecting much from foreign nations because we hadn't asked for it. I do expect a lot of sympathy and perhaps some will send cash dollars. But this country's going to rise up and take care of it. You know, we would love help, but we're going to take care of our own business as well, and there's no doubt in my mind we'll succeed. And there's no doubt in my mind, as I sit here talking to you, that New Orleans is going to rise up again as a great city.'

A lot of that aid came from the damn communists like Cuba and Venezuela, and America doesn't need help from a bunch of damn communists!

You're right. New Orleans, Myanmar — we don't need no stinkin' aid!

"As the journal *Foreign Policy* put it, 'When France and dozens of other countries pledged hundreds of millions of dollars in cash and supplies to the relief effort, their donations should have helped ease the crisis. Instead, one year after Katrina battered the Gulf Coast, none of the money given to the federal government has made its way to evacuees.'"

What do you have to say about the French now, monsieur?

Communist!

"Investigations by engineers and journalists ultimately revealed that the flooding in the city was caused, not by the strength of the hurricane, but by the weakness of the levees. These levees were designed and built by the United States Army Corps of Engineers. They were not constructed to the specifications of the designs. 'This is the first time that the Corps has had to stand up and say, we've had a catastrophic failure,'" the Corps chief said in June 2006.

Sometimes, God works through levees.

"Almost all New Orleanians were forced to evacuate in the days following Hurricane Katrina. Many thought the city would never recover and at least one Congressman suggested that New Orleans be left for dead. Yet, the city has stunned its doubters and returned to more than half its pre-storm population of roughly 450,000.

"There was particular concern that the African American community would not return, but black New Orleanians still form the majority of the city's population, albeit a smaller one."

Thanks in part to the mayor and city council, you might add. Just when affordable housing is our most acute need, Mayor Ray Nagin, Arnie Fielkow, Cynthia Willard Lewis, Jackie Clarkson, James Carter, Shelly Midura, Stacy Head and Cynthia Hedge Morrell, decided to destroy the very public housing developments where so many New Orleanians lived. May the stench of their deeds ever perfume their path!

The old buildings are being replaced with newer, better ones.

Yes, and they'll be ready for occupancy in only three years.

8

I am told that there are cities where the citizens speak with one voice and are able to achieve progress in an ordered, mature fashion. In these places, the streets are clean, the people are well-mannered and the humors of the blood are kept in passionless balance.

I am tempted by such places. If only New Orleans could tame the unruly voices within it — if only I could tame the cacophonous conflicts within myself — perhaps we and I could achieve the bland efficiency that responsible outsiders so earnestly wish for us.

But what does the music sound like in those places? What spices do they use to season their food? What sorts of colors do they paint their houses? When a street parade erupts in their path, do they honk their horns or do they get out of their cars and join in?

It's expensive living here. We pay a high tax for our nonconformity. I would gladly move, but I fear my time here has ruined me for life anywhere else. When a brass band parades in front of my house in the middle of the night, I'm neither surprised nor disturbed.

If you live long enough with these voices, they start making sense.

"It looks like a lot of that place could be bulldozed."

House Speaker Dennis Hastert (R–IL),
August 31, 2005

I think there is no country in the world so dreary and oppressive as the country round New Orleans. It is a vast swamp, below the level of the Mississippi, covered with cedars, not evergreen, but deciduous; and when I was there in the early spring, there was not a single leaf upon them. For miles these dreary forests extend, with almost always the same aspect, except, perhaps, for a few miles the trees may be bathed in yellow slimy mud half-way up their trunks, where some lake or river has been swelled and risen for a time some ten or fifteen feet higher than usual.

A Dull Life

BARBARA BODICHON
Macmillan's Magazine, May 1867

Natural scenery, untouched by man, has, almost everywhere in the world, some beauty; not always a lovely, graceful beauty, but a beautiful dreariness or a beautiful wildness, or a beautiful quaintness, or a beautiful luxuriance. Here, in this swampy, slimy Louisiana, there is ugly dreariness, ugly wildness, ugly quaintness, and the country often struck me as absolutely ugly, and, with its alligators basking in the rivers, as almost revolting, somewhat as if it were a country in a geological period not prepared for man's appearance.

We were in New Orleans in 1858, and the state of society was not more pleasant to contemplate than the natural scenery; the moral atmosphere was as offensive as the swamp miasma. Every day we heard of murders and assassinations in the streets, and crime ruled in society. The fear of vengeance from criminals very often prevented the injured from seeking the protection of the law — in fact, the state of the city was almost lawless. The aspect of the streets was quiet enough, perhaps, with the exception of a few drunken Irish and Germans, whom I saw sometimes absolutely rolling on the pavement; but it was impossible to speak to any person without hearing of recent crime, and the daily papers were crammed with revolting records.

I detested New Orleans; I detested the great Hotel St. Charles, with its 800 people sitting down to table together; and I detested the conversation I heard there at dinner, and in the immense drawing-room crowded with fine ladies. Fine gives no idea how fine these planters' ladies were; indeed, much more extravagantly dressed than crowned heads in old countries, and some wore more jewels in the early morning than a princess would wear in any evening in England. Everything I saw in New Orleans disgusted me. I could not visit the slave auction or slave depôts without suffering with horror for days after; and I could not look at the daily paper, with its little black running negroes heading innumerable advertisements of runaways, without feeling sick with sympathy for the sufferings of these human beings so indicated.

In fact, I never lost the feeling of the presence of slavery. It met me everywhere; its influence was felt everywhere: in the book-shops; in the pulpit, by the doctrines doctored to please the congregation; in the cars, by the division of white and black; in the schools, from the absence of every child supposed to have a tinge of black blood; in the evening, by the gun to send all coloured people home — everywhere, at every time, the presence of slavery was heavy upon me.

The conversations at that time, in almost all groups of people, were directly or indirectly about slavery and the infamy of the North; this infamy all connected with the peculiar institution. One evening we went to the only scientific society in the city — a poor, struggling, ill-supported association — and the interest of the lecture I heard there turned, too, on slavery. It went to prove that the Egyptians had negro slaves, and that these African races from all time had been *servants*, and always ought to be, and always would be.

There was quite enough in this city to make the heart of man sad; and though the country around was sad too, there is always the sky when one is out of the narrow streets. So I often used to go by the railway to different points in the woods, or on the Lake Pontchartrain, to get the refreshment of the beautiful sky and the gorgeous setting sun.

One day I went to Carrolton, a collection of white wooden villas, with green verandahs and gardens, very ugly and utterly uninteresting, but it is on the very verge of the uncultivated, untouched forest swamp. It was, in fact, one of the few places where it was possible to get a view of that melancholy country, and so one day, very near to Carrolton, I encamped with my sketching umbrella, &c., to make a view of the monotonous wall of deciduous cedars which rose beyond the one field which had been cleared, and cultivation attempted, but unsuccessfully; and this field, which was my foreground, was now a swamp covered with rank grass, dwarf palm, and dead stalks of tall plants. The trees beyond were leafless, but clothed in waving garments from the topmost branches to the ground, of grey moss — monotonous and fantastic.

The first day, I had not been seated more than half an hour, in dead stillness when I heard steps close behind me, and, looking up, saw a young lady, very pale and slender, with a timid, tired look, walking up to me, with a negro woman,

who, like most other household slaves, was rather fat, and remarkable for her ready smile and gay handkerchief, arranged
turbanlike on her head. I said at once, "Good morning," and,
as the timid young lady halted close to me, she said, "Good
day, ma'am," and then she stood behind me, for at least twenty
minutes, until I began to feel her eyes on my fingers, and to
get quite nervous; but, as she looked so pale and so very timid, I did not dare to say, "Go away; you prevent me from drawing," and so I turned round in despair, and said, "You must
find it very dull and tiring standing so long." "Oh, no! oh, no! I
could stand here all day, and never feel weary at all, I am so interested." This was said quickly, but in a very low voice. "Good
heavens!" thought I, "I hope not; this is very desperate;" and
seeing the negro squat down, reminded me it would be better
for us both if the young lady would sit down. So I pulled out
a corner of a mackintosh cloak, and said, "Pray sit down." The
young lady instantly accepted my not very politely-worded
offer, and sat down by me, saying, in a very low voice, lower
than before, "Oh, you are very kind!" The "kind" was almost
inaudible. I went on drawing. The young lady never spoke,
but watched me intensely. Half an hour passed, and I began
to wonder, but I determined not to break silence first, and so,
by my watch, which I took out and looked at, another half-
hour passed, when the silent young lady got up, and saying,
"Shall you come to-morrow?" awakened her sleeping negress,
and, being assured I should be there again the next day, said
"Good morning," and walked away. She went into a very little
wooden villa behind me, which very dull-looking little house
was now invested with interest for me, for this pale, uninteresting young lady excited my interest, she was so very quiet;
and now I had had time to examine her, I had found out she
had quite perfect features — not a fault to be found with the
lovely lines of brow, nose, and chin, with all so expression-

less, and so colourless, that no one could be struck with her beauty: it was beauty to discover for yourself by patient investigation. If there was any expression, it was pathos. She did not look open-eyed and stupid, as you may perhaps imagine the words expressionless to mean, but utterly weighed down, listless, and without any feeling, or desire, or restlessness, or pain, or pleasure, or anything. She looked as if she were *ennuyée*, and did not know it even.

The next day, unfortunately, there was what the Americans called a "young tornado" — that is to say, a little tempest — which flooded the country with its rain and tore up the trees with its winds, and it was, of course, impossible to think of sketching. I was very glad it was not an old tornado, if this was a specimen of the power of a young tornado. Two days after this the ground was still wet, but I went off by rail to Carrolton, and, in India-rubber boots, waded to my sketching place. Before I was installed even, my pale young lady came out of her little bathing-machine-like house, with her negress, and walked up to me with her, "Good day, ma'am." The negress said, "Oh! I be very glad you come, for Miss Cecilia sat all day at the window for three days, looking for de fine weather. I don't know what she do if you don't come."

I was touched, and said, "Miss Cecilia must have very little to do, if she has so much time to think about my drawing."

Miss Cecilia blushed a little, and said very low, "I have nothing to do."

This was said in perfect good faith, and so quietly, and so much as if it were a matter of course, that I was quite staggered.

"Nothing to do? nothing to do?" I said, accented as a question.

"Nothing to do," she answered quietly.

Then we sat down as before, in silence, and I gave her a

seat on my mackintosh and two air cushions, and made her very comfortable; and there we sat in silence.

The negress had gone into the house saying, "You will take care of Miss Cecilia," and not waiting for my answer.

Miss Cecilia sat with her hands (which were enveloped in little white cotton gloves) folded over her knees, and leaned forward, watching me intensely — watching the brush as it went into cobalt and emerald, green and sepia, and pink madder, trying hard to get the strange grey of the shroud-like moss.

I did not look up, but I felt her eyes, and gradually I lost my power of concentration on my work, and inwardly gave it up and determined to gratify my curiosity about my strange Cecilia; but I went on pretending to work and not looking at her.

"Miss Cecilia," said I, "do you paint?"

"No," said she.

"Do you sing?"

"No," said she.

"Do you ride on horseback?"

"No, no," said she.

"Do you write many letters?"

"None," said she.

"Do you like embroidery?"

"No," said she.

"Do you like crochet?"

"I do it, but I don't think I like it."

You must not think this was a brisk conversation — very far from it — there was a long gap after each "No;" and it was only the last sentence which gave me any hope of a conversation.

"What do you like?" said I.

"I do not know," said she, very low and languidly.

"But I am sure you like sitting here with me, Cecilia," said I, boldly calling her by her Christian name.

"Yes," she answered, "*very*, very much."

"Ah," rejoined I, "I am very glad that you like it very, *very* much; and you like it very, *very* much, why? tell me?"

"Oh, because it amuses me to see you take so much trouble about what I can't understand. There is nothing to draw. Why don't you draw our house? And what did you come here for? nobody ever came here before like you."

I was delighted to explain to her as well as I could a traveller's reasons for sketching, but she evidently did not really comprehend or sympathise with what I said.

Whilst I was talking, a negro woman came up to me and said, "My missus says you're to bring what you're doing to her to look at, and you're to come to the back door."

I hardly understood this message, and said so: "I don't know what your mistress wants, but if it is to look at my drawing tell her to come to me."

"Oh, I dar'n't say that; you must come along; you're to go in at the back kitchen door."

Now I confess I was a little angry and refused to go, which was very childish, for if I had had the sense to have submitted quietly I should have seen something of another family of slave-owners, and perhaps have been about to give this great lady a little lesson, but I was insulted by this continual contempt which I found any kind of steady work was exposed to. Perhaps, if this had been the first time a fine lady had treated me like a slave, because I worked like a slave, I would not have been angry; but it was the last touch which quite overset my good humour, and I shall for ever regret it. Ah, what a pity I did not go to that back kitchen-door! What I should have seen and heard must remain for ever unseen and unheard because I was put out of temper by a very natural message considering where I was and who sent it. I had the satisfaction of seeing the lady leaning out of an upper window of her house trying to see me, and Cecilia told me she was very rich and had a great many slaves, and was very cruel sometimes when she was ill and irritable.

Cecilia, after a long silence, for I was cross and quiet, said, "I want to know how you dared to go into the cypress wood the other day — are you not afraid of the runaway slaves there? They say they are worse than wild beasts."

"Oh no; there can't be any so close to the town. I was not afraid; I only went for a little walk. Don't you ever go for a walk?"

"No, never."

This reminded me of a fashionable young lady in New Orleans, who had never seen the country at all round her city, and who did not know of what we were speaking when we spoke of the long grey moss one day at a dinner party. I told my companion this, and she said, "Oh, she had seen it, no doubt, in the shops ready for stuffing mattresses, and thought it was horse-hair! But I am not astonished she had not seen it in the country: why should she go to see it?"

I tried to make her understand the many reasons — moral, physical, and intellectual — why we should take walks in the country, or rides, or drives, or all three; but I suppose my disquisition was very dull, for she did not seem to care about it, and fell into her listless attitude. So after a little silence I fell into the cross-questioning method, which was the only possible one with my strange companion.

"Have you always lived here?"

"No, we lived in New Orleans when I was little and my parents were alive. Since their death I have always lived there with grandmother," said she, pointing to the green and white box.

66

Then, in answer to my questions, she told me she was twenty, and that her father and mother had died of yellow fever when she was five years old and her only brother seven; that she had doted on, and adored her brother John; that he had been quite different from her, very lively and very clever; and that he could not bear to live a quiet life, so he ran away from home and had joined General Walker, who was his great hero, and had been killed in Nicaragua. She told me how a letter came to her grandmother and she had to read it as her grandmother was too blind, and how, after understanding the terrible news, she fell down in a faint and was sick for weeks and weeks after. "But," said she wearily, "that is six years ago; a very long time ago." She went on to tell me, that her grandmother was very old and infirm, and now quite blind, that she was very kind and very good, but that she would never let her go out anywhere, because it cost money, nor learn the piano, or sing, because that cost money too, and because she could not bear a noise or bustle in the house: the rooms being divided with wood only, you could hear every sound in the house as if it were one room.

"She is very good to me," said Cecilia. "She has a little money; and as my father died in debt, it is very good of her to keep me. She says I and my brother have cost her a great deal of money."

"If she said that," said I to myself, "I do not think she has been very good to you, and it is fortunate for you if you think so."

"She is a great sufferer now," continued Cecilia, "and Zoe has to sit by her for hours, holding her hands or combing her hair, and sometimes for days she will not see me. She does not believe I know how to nurse or do anything. Zoe is a very good creature: I should not be here now, but Zoe has the sense to say, when grandmother asks where I am, 'Miss Cecil is close by; I can see her.'"

I sat silently wondering at this dull life, and thinking of all the avenues to activity in any little town in England for a young lady like Cecilia — the church, the chapel, the little social societies for charity, all of which occupy those who are too poor or too pious for balls, picnics, and country gaieties. We have in England so many small organizations that it would be strange there to find a being who did not deliberately choose it, leading so isolated a life as my poor Cecilia. In England the clergymen or the minister and the doctor are the steady friends of the most solitary woman.

"Do you not go to church?" I said.

"Sometimes, but not very often. Grandmamma will not let me go alone; and as she likes the minister to come and read prayers to her, I stay with her; but I like to go to the church best, because I like to see the people."

"But don't you see any one — not the doctor?" said I, determined to find out if this life were really so cut off from all human fellowship as it seemed.

"Oh, sometimes we do see the doctor."

Cecilia blushed deeply with some emotions or other, as she mentioned the doctor, so I asked her if she liked her grandmother's doctor.

"Oh yes, very well," said she.

But this did not satisfy me, and I put ingenious questions, which it would be very tedious to relate, until I extracted the following episode in her life.

Two years ago, in the middle of the summer, there had been a terrible attack of yellow fever, which had been more than usually fatal; the deaths followed so quickly — hundreds upon hundreds — that a deadly panic seized the people, and in many places the doctors and horses fled. Hospitals were obliged to be hastily prepared where the rich and poor were taken alike. The doctor, Cecilia's friend, had under his care a hospital for children, which was the schoolhouse, hastily adapted to its new purpose. The long rows of desks and forms were covered with mattresses, and children in every stage of the disease were crowded together: some were nursed by relations, but the greater part by ladies who volunteered to do what few women dared to do for hire. This doctor had taken Cecilia, in spite of her grandmother's disapprobation, and put her into this hospital, where it was evident he had soon felt her worth, for he had made her, young as she was, chief of a wing. He had praised her devotedness, he had depended upon her, he had called her his Sister of Charity, and entrusted many difficult missions to her care; she had found out what liberty was; for she had been about alone on the business of the hospital and found herself full of courage and life. She was intensely grateful to the man who had made her useful and found her good for something, and she had evidently regarded the doctor as the good angel of her life. He had made a mark in her life; but she, alas! had not, it seemed, occupied his attention after the pestilence had passed. He was, probably a very busy man, and had almost forgotten her; he did remember her, indeed, sometimes; but he was too full of his own family affairs, his patients, and his negroes, to think much of his devoted Cecilia.

"Ah!" said she, with the longest sigh I ever heard, "I don't know how it was, and of course it is very wicked, but I never was so happy in all my life! Every day I was up at four and never in bed until twelve, and the more I did the stronger I was; but now I do nothing all day I am very weak."

"But don't you visit the doctor's wife?"

"No; his wife is a fine lady, and I cannot dress so well as she does, so I do not like to go; people here think a great deal about dress. If you can't dress you can't visit the planters' families and the doctor's family is quite a fashionable family. I am too poor, in reality, to go among such people."

"Then, why did not your grandmother give you a good education so that you might give lessons and earn money, as you can never be in what you call fashionable society?"

"Oh," said Cecilia, "she is too proud for that; and besides, all the governesses and teachers come from the North, and I never could have been so clever and accomplished as they are."

Then she told me about the planters who lived in the great houses, and the retired storekeepers of New Orleans who lived in little villas around us. She said they were very proud indeed; that they did just bow to her in passing, that was all, though many of them had known her and her grandmother for fifteen years. She said her grandmother had been quite well know, and had eight hundred slaves.

"You have only Zoe now?" I said.

"Only Zoe," said she; "but Zoe is married and has had four children."

"And where are they?" asked I, with a certain shuddering curiosity.

"They are all gone away."

"Sold?" said I, with my heart aching within me.

"Yes," said Cecilia, quite quietly, with no emotion.

"But don't you think it wrong of your grandmother to sell another woman's children?" said I, hotly and boldly — too boldly considering I was in Louisiana, where a less bold speech has been punished with tar and feathers.

"Zoe's children?" said she, not understanding my implication at all.

"Yes," said I; "Zoe is a woman! Zoe's children!"

Cecilia looked at me with eyes wide open, quite astonished, and said, "But, you see, grandmamma could not afford to keep five people, and she wanted money; so, of course, she sold them. What should you have done with them?"

Here was a puzzling question! Cecilia looked at me as if she could not guess in the least my thought. I think she rather imagined I was proposing they should be drowned as kittens — these unhappy black babies; she had no idea, certainly that any one could think there was a responsibility somewhere to bring them up as Christian children. I did not attempt to answer her questions, for I am sure I did not know what I should have done with them; but I asked her another, "Do you not think it wrong to have slaves?"

"I never though about it; does any one think it wrong?"

Here was an opportunity for argument, and I hardly knew how to begin, so I hazarded, "Have you read *Uncle Tom's Cabin?*"

"No, never," said she. "I have not read many books, for, as grandmother is blind, she won't buy any books. I have read the Bible all through, but I do not remember anything about slavery being wrong in it."

I entered into the subject heart and soul, and told her there were millions of people who thought slavery wrong; and I told her how England had freed her slaves, and how work was done better for fair pay than fear; and how the labourer, who was free, was respected, and the effect of this respect for work on all people — ladies and gentlemen and all. She became so intensely interested in this new idea that I was afraid she might speak out imprudently, so I cautioned her and told her of the experience of some of my abolitionist friends. Her face lighted up, and her beautiful eyes kindled as I told her how many women had suffered for saying that they thought slavery wrong. I went on to tell her of Miss M. G. and others who had been born slave-owners and rich, and who had freed all their slaves and lived a life of hard work and poverty rather than have any share in what they conceived to be a great iniquity.

"Supposing you are right that slavery is wrong, what will happen to us here? Shall we be treated like Sodom and Gomorrah?"

I told her I thought that by God's laws, as we knew them, society could not be peaceful, constituted as this was in opposition to His evident intentions; that I did not think she need fear fire or brimstone, but that she must look for some change; what it would be I could not tell. It was getting late, and the damp mist was rising, so I was obliged to go. I walked with Cecilia to her door, kissed her, and promised to come the next day. Alas! the next day we received sad news from England, and we were obliged to start immediately for Mobile on our way home.

I had no regrets in leaving New Orleans except in causing some sorrow to some poor negro friends of ours, and the one deep regret of being unable to fulfil my engagement with poor Cecilia — poor, poor Cecilia! It was sad for her to lose her new friend, and it seemed as if her life was doomed to sadness and disappointment. I tormented myself with the imagination of this lonely figure standing waiting in the marsh, and longing for the strange visitor to come and continue the conversation which had just begun to be so intimate, affectionate, and interesting. I thought of her going home to the dull house and the dull inmates. I was grieved to the heart to think of her daily bitter disappointments, and I was then provoked and sorry I had not given her my name and address, for she really did not know my name; it was a tormenting pain to me the whole of my journey; and though I had written to her before leaving, and sent her a parcel of books, I had not faith enough in the post of Louisiana to believe she would ever receive the letter or the packet. In my letter I begged of her to write me at New York and also to London. Alas! there was no letter at New York. I wrote again to her with no result. Weeks passed, we arrived in England, but never a letter has come to me from Cecilia. At the beginning of the war I wrote to her again, but I have never received any answer. Great changes have taken place in New Orleans since I was there, and I have this satisfaction in thinking of Cecilia, that whatever change has taken place in her fate, must be for the better. She is dead, perhaps; she has fallen in with some Federal officer who may love her; or she is again a hospital nurse. There is little doubt that she is happier now than when she sat beside me that first day I met her; probably, the ideas I gave her were thought over and over in her mind, and she was prepared for what has happened and ready for the time of change.

The life of this poor young lady in Louisiana was the dullest life I ever knew — dull, because her domestic life happened to be sad, lonely; dull, because she was poor; dull, because she was in a slave State; dull, because the country was dull and dreary; dull, because she was a young lady with nothing to do and very little education. Happily, such a dull life is not possible in many countries, and was rare no doubt in the country where I came across it.

Ask an informed American citizen today to ruminate on Dallas or Atlanta or Phoenix, and you will probably get small talk, lukewarm pleasantries, and a brief conversation. Ask them what they think about New Orleans, and you are in for not only an opinionated retort, but a sentimental smile, a scolding finger, a treasured memory, a shaking head, or an exasperated shrug over the course of a conversation spanning the spectrum of human experience. This enigmatic capacity to rile and inspire, to scandalize and charm, to liberate and fascinate, helps explain why thousands of people have rejected the amenities and opportunities of the lukewarm Dallases and Atlantas and Phoenixes of the world, and chosen instead to cast their lot with this troubled old port — embracing all its splendors and dilemmas, all its booms and busts, all it joys and tragedies.

Because thou art lukewarm, and neither hot nor cold,
I spew thee from my mouth.

Revelation 3:16

from Richard Campanella
Bienville's Dilemma (2008)

The first time I saw New Orleans was on a Sunday morning in the month of March. We alighted from the train at the foot of Esplanade Street, and walked along through the French Market, and by Jackson Square to the Hotel Royal. The morning, after rain, was charming; there was a fresh breeze from the river; the foliage was a tender green; in the balconies and on the mouldering window-ledges flowers bloomed, and in the decaying courts climbing-roses mingled their perfume with the orange; the shops were open; ladies tripped along from early mass or to early market; there was a twittering in the square and in the sweet old gardens; caged birds sang and

New Orleans

CHARLES DUDLEY WARNER

Harper's New Monthly Magazine, January 1887

screamed the songs of South America and the tropics; the language heard on all sides was French, or the degraded jargon which the easy-going African has manufactured out of the tongue of Bienville. Nothing could be more shabby than the streets, ill-paved, with undulating sidewalks, and open gutters green with slime, and both stealing and giving odor; little canals in which the cat became the companion of the crawfish, and the vegetable in decay sought in vain a current to oblivion; the streets with rows of one-story houses, wooden, with green doors and batten window-shutters, or brick, with the painted stucco peeling off, the line broken often by an edifice of two stories, with galleries and delicate tracery of wrought iron, houses pink and yellow and brown and gray — colors all blending and harmonious when we get a long vista of them, and lose the details of view in the broad artistic effect; nothing could be shabbier than the streets, unless it is the tumble-down picturesque old market, bright with flowers and vegetables and many-hued fish, and enlivened by the genial African, who in the New World experiments in all colors, from coal-black to the pale pink of the sea-shell, to find one that suits his mobile nature. I liked it all from the first; I lingered long in that morning walk, liking it more and more, in spite of its shabbiness, but utterly unable to say then or ever since wherein its charm lies. I suppose we are all wrongly made up and have a fallen nature; else why is it that while the most thrifty and neat and orderly city only wins our approval, and perhaps gratifies us intellectually, such a thriftless, battered and stained, and lazy old place as the French quarter of New Orleans takes our hearts?

I never could find out exactly where New Orleans is. I have looked for it on the map without much enlightenment. It is dropped down there somewhere in the marshes of the Mississippi and the bayous and lakes. It is below the one and tangled up among the others, or it might some day float out to the Gulf and disappear. How the Mississippi gets out I never could discover. When it first comes in sight of the town it is running east; at Carrollton it abruptly turns its rapid, broad, yellow flood and runs south, turns presently eastward, circles a great portion of the city, then makes a bold push for the north in order to avoid Algiers and reach the foot of Canal Street, and encountering then the heart of the town, it sheers off again along the old French quarter and Jackson Square due east, and goes no one knows where, except perhaps Mr. Eads.

The city is supposed to lie in this bend of the river, but it in fact extends eastward along the bank down to the Barracks, and spreads backward toward Lake Pontchartrain over a vast area, and includes some very good snipe-shooting.

Although New Orleans has only about a quarter of a million of inhabitants, and so many only in the winter, it is larger than Pekin, and I believe than Philadelphia, having an area of about one hundred and five square miles. From Carrollton to the Barracks, which are not far from the Battle-Field, the distance by the river is some thirteen miles. From the river to the lake the least distance is four miles. This vast territory is traversed by lines of horse-cars which all meet in Canal Street, the most important business thoroughfare of the city, which runs northeast from the river and divides the French from the American quarter. One taking a horse-car in any part of the city will ultimately land, having boxed the compass, in Canal Street. But it needs a person of vast local erudition to tell in what part of the city, or in what section of the home of the frog and crawfish, he will land if he takes a horse-car in Canal Street. The river being higher than the city, there is of course no drainage into it; but there is a theory that the water in the open gutters does move, and that it moves in the direction of the Bayou St. John, and of the cypress swamps that drain into Lake Pontchartrain. The stranger who is accustomed to closed sewers, and to get his malaria and typhoid through pipes conducted into his house by the most approved methods of plumbing, is aghast at this spectacle of slime and filth in the streets, and wonders why the city is not in perennial epidemic; but the sun and the wind are great scavengers, and the city is not nearly so unhealthy as it ought to be with such a city government as they say it endures.

It is not necessary to dwell much upon the external features of New Orleans, for innumerable descriptions and pictures have familiarized the public with them. Besides, descriptions can give the stranger little idea of the peculiar city. Although all on one level, it is a town of contrasts. In no other city of the United States or of Mexico is the old and the romantic preserved in such integrity and brought into such sharp contrast to the modern. There are many handsome public buildings, churches, clubhouses, elegant shops, and on the American side a great area of well-paved streets solidly built up in business blocks. The Square of the original city, included between the river and canal, Rampart and Esplanade streets, which was once surrounded by a wall, is as closely built, but the streets are narrow, the houses generally are smaller, and although it swarms with people, and contains the cathedral, the old Spanish buildings, Jackson Square, the French Market, the French Opera-house and other theatres, the Mint, the Custom-house, the old Ursuline Convent (now the residence of the archbishop), old banks, and scores of houses of historic celebrity, it is a city of the past, and specially interesting in its picturesque decay. Beyond this, eastward and northward extend interminable streets of small houses, with now and then a flowery court or a pretty rose garden, occupied mainly by people of French and Spanish descent. The African pervades all parts of the town, except the new residence portion of the American quarter. This, which occupies the vast area in the bend of the river west of the business blocks as far as Carrollton, is in character a great village rather than a city. Not all its broad avenues and handsome streets are paved (and those that are not are in some seasons impassable), its houses are nearly all of wood, most of them detached, with plots of ground and gardens, and as the quarter is very well shaded, the effect is bright and agreeable. In it are many stately residences, occupying a square or half a square, and embowered in foliage and flowers. Care has been given

lately to turf-culture, and one sees here thick-set and handsome lawns. The broad Esplanade Street, with its elegant old-
fashioned houses, and double rows of shade trees, which has
long been the rural pride of the French quarter, has now rivals
in respectability and style on the American side.

New Orleans is said to be delightful in the late fall months,
before the winter rains set in, but I believe it looks its best
in March and April. This is owing to the roses. If the town
was not attached to the name of the Crescent City, it might
very well adopt the title of the City of Roses. So kind are
climate and soil that the magnificent varieties of this queen
of flowers, which at the North bloom only in hot-houses, or
with great care are planted outdoors in the heat of our summer, thrive here in the open air in prodigal abundance and
beauty. In April the town is literally embowered in them; they
fill door-yards and gardens, they overrun the porches, they
climb the sides of the houses, they spread over the trees, they
take possession of trellises and fences and walls, perfuming
the air and entrancing the heart with color. In the outlying
parks, like that of the Jockey Club, and the florists' gardens at
Carrollton, there are fields of them, acres of the finest sorts,
waving in the spring wind. Alas! can beauty ever satisfy? This
wonderful spectacle fills one with I know not what exquisite
longing. These flowers pervade the town, old women on the
street corners sit behind banks of them, the florists' windows blush with them, friends despatch to each other great
baskets of them, the favorites at the theatre and the amateur
performers stand behind high barricades of roses which the
good-humored audience piles upon the stage, everybody
carries roses and wears roses, and the houses overflow with
them. In this passion for flowers you may read a prominent
trait of the people. For myself I like to see a spot on this earth
where beauty is enjoyed for itself and let to run to waste, but

if ever the industrial spirit of the French-Italians should prevail along the littoral of Louisiana and Mississippi, the raising of flowers for the manufacture of perfumes would become a most profitable industry.

New Orleans is the most cosmopolitan of provincial cities. Its comparative isolation has secured the development of provincial traits and manners, has preserved the individuality of the many races that give it color, morals, and character while its close relations with France — an affiliation and sympathy which the late-war has not altogether broken — and the constant influx of Northern men of business and affairs, have given it the air of a metropolis. To the Northern stranger the aspect and the manners of the city are foreign, but if he remains long enough he is sure to yield to its fascinations, and become a partisan of it. It is not altogether the soft and somewhat enervating and occasionally treacherous climate that beguiles him, but quite as much the easy terms on which life can be lived. There is a human as well as a climatic amiability that wins him. No doubt it is better for a man to be always braced up, but no doubt also there is an attraction in a complaisance that indulges his inclinations.

Socially as well as commercially New Orleans is in a transitive state. The change from river to railway transportation has made her levees vacant; the shipment of cotton by rail and its direct transfer to ocean carriage have nearly destroyed a large middle-men industry; a large part of the agricultural tribute of the Southwest has been diverted; plantations have either not recovered from the effects of the war or have not adjusted themselves to new productions, and the city waits the rather blind developments of the new era. The falling off of law business, which I should like to attribute to the growth of common-sense and good-will, is, I fear, rather due to business lassitude, for it is observed that men quarrel most when they are most actively engaged in acquiring each other's property. The business habits of the Creoles were conservative and slow, they do not readily accept new ways, and in this transition time the American element is taking the lead in all enterprises. The American element itself is toned down by the climate and the contagion of the leisurely habits of the Creoles, and loses something of the sharpness and excitability exhibited by business men in all Northern cities, but it is certainly changing the social as well as the business aspect of the city. Whether these social changes will make New Orleans a more agreeable place of residence remains to be seen.

For the old civilization had many admirable qualities. With all its love of money and luxury and an easy life, it was comparatively simple. It cared less for display than the society that is supplanting it. Its rule was domesticity. I should say that it had the virtues as well as the prejudices and the narrowness of intense family feeling, and its exclusiveness. But when it trusted, it had few reserves, and its cordiality was equal to its *naïveté*. The Creole civilization differed totally from that in any Northern city; it looked at life, literature, wit, manners, from altogether another plane; in order to understand the society of New Orleans one needs to imagine what French society would be in a genial climate and in the freedom of a new country. Undeniably, until recently, the Creoles gave the tone to New Orleans. And it was the French culture, the French view of life, that was diffused. The young ladies mainly were educated in convents and French schools. This education had womanly agreeability and matrimony in view, and the graces of social life. It differed not much from the education of young ladies of the period elsewhere, except that it was from the French rather than the English side, but this made a world of difference. French was a study and a possession, not a fashionable accomplishment. The Creole had gayety, sentiment, spirit, with a certain climatic languor, sweetness of disposition, and charm of manner, not seldom winning beauty; she was passionately fond of dancing and of music, and occasionally an adept in the latter; and she had candor, and either simplicity or the art of it. But with her tendency to domesticity and her capacity for friendship, and notwithstanding her gay temperament, she was less worldly than some of her sisters who were more gravely educated after the English manner. There was therefore in the old New Orleans life something nobler than the spirit of plutocracy. The Creole middle-class population had, and has yet, captivating *naïveté*, friendliness, cordiality.

But the Creole influence in New Orleans is wider and deeper than this. It has affected literary sympathies and what may be called literary morals. In business the Creole is accused of being slow, conservative, in regard to improvements obstinate and reactionary, preferring to nurse a prejudice rather than run the risk of removing it by improving himself, and of having a conceit that his way of looking at life is better than the Boston way. His literary culture is derived from France, and not from England or the North. And his ideas a good deal affect the attitude of New Orleans toward English and contemporary literature. The American element of the town was for the most part commercial, arid, little given to literary tastes. That also is changing, but I fancy it is still true that the most solid culture is with the Creoles, and it has not been appreciated because it is French, and because its point of view for literary criticism is quite different from that prevailing elsewhere in America. It brings our American and English contemporary authors, for instance, to comparison, not with each other, but with French and other Continental writers. And this point of view considerably affects the New Orleans opinion of Northern literature. In this view it wants color, passion, it is too self-conscious and prudish, not to say Puritanically mock-modest. I do not mean to say that the Creoles as a class are a reading people, but the literary standards of their scholars and of those among them who do cultivate literature deeply are different from those at the North. We may call it provincial, or we may call it cosmopolitan, but we shall not understand New Orleans until we get its point of view of both life and letters.

In making these observations it will occur to the reader that they are of necessity superficial, and not entitled to be regarded as criticism or judgment. But I am impressed with the foreignness of New Orleans civilization, and whether its point of view is right or wrong, I am very far from wishing it to change. It contains a valuable element of variety for the republic. We tend everywhere to sameness and monotony. New Orleans is entering upon a new era of development, especially in educational life. The Toulane University is beginning to make itself felt as a force both in polite letters and in industrial education. And I sincerely hope that the literary development of the city and of the Southwest will be in the line of its own traditions, and that it will not be a copy of New England or of Dutch Manhattan. It can, if it is faithful to its own sympathies and temperament, make an original and valuable contribution to our literary life.

There is a great temptation to regard New Orleans through the romance of its past; and the most interesting occupation of the idler is to stroll about in the French part of the town, search the shelves of French and Spanish literature in the second-hand book-shops, try to identify the historic sites and the houses that are the seats of local romances, and observe the life in the narrow streets and alleys that, except for the presence of the colored folk, recall the quaint picturesqueness of many a French provincial town. One never tires of wandering in the neighborhood of the old cathedral, facing the smart Jackson Square, which is flanked by the respectable Pontalba buildings, and supported on either side by the ancient Spanish court-house, the most interesting specimens of Spanish architecture this side of Mexico. When the court is in session, iron cables are stretched across the street to prevent the passage of wagons, and justice is administered in silence only broken by the trill of birds in the Place d'Armes and in the old flower-garden in the rear of the cathedral, and by the muffled sound of footsteps in the flagged passages. The region is saturated with romance, and so full of present sentiment and picturesqueness that I can fancy no ground more congenial to the artist and the story-teller. To enter into any details of it would be to commit one's self to a task quite foreign to the purpose of this paper, and I leave it to the writers who have done and are doing so much to make old New Orleans classic.

Possibly no other city of the United States so abounds in stories pathetic and tragic, many of which cannot yet be published, growing out of the mingling of races, the conflicts of French and Spanish, the presence of adventurers from the Old World and the Spanish Main, and especially out of the relations between the whites and the fair women who had in their thin veins drops of African blood. The quadroon and the octoroon are the staple of hundreds of thrilling tales. Duels were common incidents of the Creole dancing assemblies, and of the *cordon bleu* balls — the deities of which were the quadroon women, "the handsomest race of women in the world," says the description, and the most splendid dancers and the most exquisitely dressed — the affairs of honor being settled by a midnight thrust in a vacant square behind the cathedral, or adjourned to a more French daylight encounter at "The Oaks," or "Les Trois Capalins." But this life has all gone.

In a stately building in this quarter, said by tradition to have been the quadroon ball-room, but I believe it was a white assembly-room connected with the opera, is now a well-ordered school for colored orphans, presided over by colored Sisters of Charity.

It is quite evident that the peculiar prestige of the quadroon and the octoroon is a thing of the past. Indeed, the war has greatly changed the relations of the two races in New Orleans. The colored people withdraw more and more to themselves. Isolation from white influence has good results and bad results, the bad being, as one can see, in some quarters of the town, a tendency to barbarism, which can only be counteracted by free public schools, and by a necessity which shall compel them to habits of thrift and industry. One needs to be very much an optimist, however, to have patience for these developments.

I believe there is an instinct in both races against mixture of blood, and upon this rests the law of Louisiana, which forbids such intermarriages; the time may come when the colored people will be as strenuous in insisting upon its execution as the whites, unless there is a great change in popular feeling, of which there is no sign at present; it is they who will see that there is no escape from the equivocal position in which those nearly white in appearance find themselves except by a rigid separation of races. The danger is of a reversal at any time to the original type, and that is always present to the offspring of any one with a drop of African blood in the veins. The pathos of this situation is infinite, and it cannot be lessened by saying that the prejudice about color is unreasonable; it exists. Often the African strain is so attenuated that the possessor of it would pass to the ordinary observer for Spanish or French; and I suppose that many so-called Creole peculiarities of speech and manner are traceable to this strain.

An incident in point may not be uninteresting.

I once lodged in the old French quarter in a house kept by two maiden sisters, only one of whom spoke English at all. They were refined, and had the air of decayed gentlewomen. The one who spoke English had the vivacity and agreeability of a Paris landlady, without the latter's invariable hardness and sharpness. I thought I had found in her pretty mode of speech the real Creole dialect of her class. "You are French," I said, when I engaged my room.

"No," she said, "no, m'sieu, I am an American; we are of the United States," with the air of informing a stranger that New Orleans was now annexed.

"Yes," I replied, "but you are of French descent?"

"Oh, and a little Spanish."

"Can you tell me, madame," I asked, one Sunday morning, "the way to Trinity Church?"

"I cannot tell, m'sieu; it is somewhere the other side; I do not know the other side."

"But have you never been the other side of Canal Street?"

"Oh yes, I went once, to make a visit on a friend on New-Year's."

I explained that it was far uptown, and a Protestant church.

"M'sieu is he Cat'olic?"

"Oh no; I am a Protestant."

"Well, me, I am Cat'olic; but Protestan' o' Cat'olic, it is 'mos' ze same."

This was purely the instinct of politeness, and that my feelings might not be wounded, for she was a good Catholic, and did not believe at all that it was "'mos' ze same."

It was Exposition year, and then April, and madame had never been to the Exposition. I urged her to go, and one day, after great preparation, she made the expedition, and returned enchanted with all she had seen, especially with the

Mexican band. A new world was opened to her, and she resolved to go again. The morning of Louisiana Day she rapped at my door and informed me that she was going to the fair. "And," she paused at the doorway, her eyes sparkling with her new project, "you know what I goin' do?"

"No."

"I goin' get one big bouquet, and give to the leader of the orchestre."

"You know him, the leader?"

"No, not yet."

I did not know then how poor she was, how much sacrifice this would be to her, this gratification of a sentiment.

The next year, in the same month, I asked for her at the lodging. She was not there. "You did not know," said the woman then in possession — "good God! Her sister died four days ago, from want of food, and madame has gone away back of town, nobody knows where. They told nobody, they were so proud; none of their friends knew, or they would have helped. They had no lodgers, and could not keep this place, and took another opposite; but they were unlucky, and the sheriff came." I said that I was very sorry that I had not known; she might have been helped. "No," she replied, with considerable spirit; "she would have accepted nothing; she would starve rather. So would I." The woman referred me to some well-known Creole families who knew madame, but I was unable to find her hiding-place. I asked who madame was. "Oh, she was a very nice woman, very respectable. Her father was Spanish, her mother was an octoroon."

One does not need to go into the past of New Orleans for the picturesque; the streets have their peculiar physiognomy, and "character" such as the artists delight to depict is the result of the extraordinary mixture of races and the habit of outdoor life. The long summer, from April to November, with a heat continuous, though rarely so excessive as it occasionally is in higher latitudes, determines the mode of life and the structure of the houses, and gives a leisurely and amiable tone to the aspect of people and streets which exists in few other American cities. The French quarter has the air of being for rent, but in fact there is comparatively little change in occupancy, Creole families being remarkably adhesive to localities. The stranger who sees all over the French and business parts of the town the immense number of lodging-houses — some of them the most stately old mansions — let largely by colored landladies, is likely to underestimate the home life of this city. New Orleans soil is so wet that the city is without cellars for storage, and its court-yards and odd corners become catch-alls of broken furniture and other lumber. The solid window-shutters, useful in the glare of the long summer, give a blank appearance to the streets. This is relieved by the queer little Spanish houses and by the endless variety of galleries and balconies. In one part of the town the iron-work of the balconies is cast, and uninteresting in its set patterns; in French-town much of it is handmade, exquisite in design, and gives to a street vista a delicate lace-work appearance. I do not know any foreign town which has on view so much exquisite wrought-iron work as the old part of New Orleans. Besides the balconies, there are recessed galleries, old dormer-windows, fantastic little nooks and corners tricked out with flower-pots and vines.

The glimpses of street life are always entertaining, because unconscious, while full of character. It may be a Creole court-yard, the walls draped with vines, flowers blooming in hap-hazard disarray, and a group of pretty girls sewing and chatting, and stabbing the passer-by with a charmed glance. It may be a cotton team in the street, the mules, the rollicking driver, the creaking cart. It may be a single figure, or a group in the market or on the levee — a slender yellow girl sweeping up the grains of rice, a colored gleaner recalling Ruth; an ancient darky asleep, with mouth open, in his tipped-up two-wheeled cart, waiting for a job; the "solid South," in shape of an immense "aunty" under a red umbrella, standing and contemplating the river; the broad-faced women in gay bandanas behind their cake stands; a group of levee hands about a rickety table, taking their noon-day meal of pork and greens; the blind man, capable of sitting more patiently than an American Congressman, with a ᴄog trained to hold his basket for the pennies of the charitable; the black stalwart vender of tin and iron utensils, who totes in a basket, and piled on his head, and strung on his back, a weight of over two hundred and fifty pounds; and negro women who walk erect with baskets of clothes or enormous bundles balanced on their heads, smiling and "jawing," unconscious of their burdens. These are the familiar figures of a street life as varied and picturesque as the artist can desire.

New Orleans amuses itself in the winter with very good theatres, and until recently has sustained an excellent French opera. It has all the year round plenty of *cafés chantants*, gilded saloons, and gambling houses, and more than enough of the resorts upon which the police are supposed to keep one blind eye. "Back of town," toward Lake Pontchartrain, there is much that is picturesque and blooming, especially in the spring of the year — the charming gardens of the Jockey Club, the City Park, the old duelling ground with its superb oaks, and the Bayou St. John with its idling fishing-boats, and the colored houses and plantations along the banks — a piece of Holland wanting the Dutch windmills. On a breezy day one may go far for a prettier sight than the river-bank and esplanade at Carrollton, where the mighty coffee-colored flood swirls by, where the vast steamers struggle and cough against the stream, or swiftly go with it round the bend, leaving their trail of smoke, and the delicate line of foliage against the sky on the far opposite shore completes the outline of an exquisite landscape. Suburban resorts much patronized, and reached by frequent trains, are the old Spanish Fort and the West End of Lake Pontchartrain. The way lies through cypress swamp and palmetto thickets, brilliant at certain seasons with *fleur-de-lis*. At each of these resorts are restaurants, dancing balls, promenade galleries, all on a large scale, boat-houses and semi-tropical gardens very prettily laid out in walks and labyrinths, and adorned with trees and flowers. Even in the heat of summer at night the lake is sure to offer a breeze, and with waltz music and moonlight and ices and tinkling glasses with straws in them and love's young dream, even the *ennuyé* globe-trotter declares that it is not half bad.

The city, indeed, offers opportunity for charming excursions in all directions. Parties are constantly made up to visit the river plantations, to sail up and down the stream, or to take an outing across the lake, or to the many lovely places along the coast. In the winter, excursions are made to these places, and in summer, the well-to-do take the sea-air in cottages, at such places as Mandeville across the lake, or at such resorts on the Mississippi as Pass Christian.

I crossed the lake one spring day to the pretty town of Mandeville, and then sailed up the Tchefuncta River to Covington. The winding Tehefuncta is in character like some of the narrow Florida streams, has the same luxuriant overhanging foliage, and as many shy lounging alligators to the mile, and is prettier by reason of occasional open glades and large moss-draped live-oaks and China-trees. From the steamer landing in the woods we drove three miles through a lovely open pine forest to the town. Covington is one of the oldest settlements in the State, is the centre of considerable historic interest, and the origin of several historic families. The land is elevated a good deal above the coast level, and is consequently dry. The town has a few roomy old-time houses, a mineral spring, some pleasing scenery along the river that winds through it, and not much else. But it is in the midst of pine woods, it is sheltered from all "northers," it has-the soft air, but not the dampness, of the Gulf, and is exceedingly salubrious in all the winter months, to say nothing of the summer. It has lately come into local repute as a health resort, although it lacks sufficient accommodations for the entertainment of many strangers. I was told by some New Orleans physicians that they regarded it as almost a specific for pulmonary diseases, and instances were given of persons in what was supposed to be advanced stages of lung and bronchial troubles who had been apparently cured by a few months' residence there; and invalids are, I believe, greatly benefited by its healing, soft, and piny atmosphere.

I have no doubt, from what I hear and my limited observation, that all this coast about New Orleans would be a favorite winter resort if it had hotels as good as, for instance, that at Pass Christian. The region has many attractions for the idler and the invalid. It is, in the first place, interesting; it has a good deal of variety of scenery and of historical interest; there is excellent fishing and shooting; and if the visitor tires of the monotony of the country, he can by a short ride on cars or a steamer transfer himself for a day or a week to a large and most hospitable city, to society, the club, the opera, balls, parties, and every variety of life that his taste craves. The disadvantage of many Southern places to which our Northern regions force us is that they are uninteresting, stupid, and monotonous, if not malarious. It seems a long way from New York to New Orleans, but I do not doubt that the region around the city would become immediately a great winter resort if money and enterprise were enlisted to make it so.

New Orleans has never been called a "strait-laced" city; its Sunday is still of the Continental type; but it seems to me free from the socialistic agnosticism which flaunts itself more or less in Cincinnati, St. Louis, and Chicago; the tone of leading Presbyterian churches is distinctly Calvinistic, one perceives comparatively little of religious speculation and doubt, and so far as I could see there is harmony and entire social good feeling between the Catholic and Protestant communions. Protestant ladies assist at Catholic fairs, and the compliment is returned by the society ladies of the Catholic faith when a Protestant good cause is to be furthered by a bazar or a "pink tea." Denominational lines seem to have little to do with social affiliations. There may be friction in the management of the great public charities, but on the surface there is toleration and united good-will. The Catholic faith long had the prestige of wealth, family, and power, and the education of the daughters of Protestant houses in convent schools tended to allay prejudice. Notwithstanding the reputation New Orleans has for gayety and even frivolity — and no one can deny the fast and furious living of ante-bellum days — it possesses at bottom an old-fashioned religious simplicity. If any one thinks that "faith" has died out of modern life, let him visit the mortuary chapel of St. Roch. In a distant part of the town, beyond the street of the Elysian Fields, and on Washington Avenue, in a district very sparsely built up, is the Campo Santo of the Catholic Church of the Holy Trinity. In this foreign-looking cemetery is the pretty little Gothic Chapel of St. Roch, having a background of common and swampy land. It is a brown stuccoed edifice, wholly open in front, and was a year or two ago covered with beautiful ivy. The small interior is paved in white marble, the windows are stained glass, the side walls are composed of tiers of vaults, where are buried the members of certain societies, and the spaces in the wall and in the altar area are thickly covered with votive offerings, in wax and in *naïve* painting — contributed by those who have been healed by the intercession of the saints. Over the altar is the shrine of St. Roch — a cavalier, staff in hand, with his dog by his side, the faithful animal which accompanied this eighth-century philanthropist in his visitations to the plague-stricken people of Munich. Within the altar rail are rows of lighted candles, tended and renewed by the attendant, placed there by penitents or by seekers after the favor of the saint. On the wooden benches, kneeling, are ladies, servants, colored women, in silent prayer. One approaches the lighted, picturesque shrine through the formal rows of tombs, and comes there into an atmosphere of peace and faith. It is believed that miracles are daily wrought here, and one notices in all the gardeners, keepers, and attendants of the place the accent and demeanor of simple faith. On the wall hangs this inscription:

O great St. Roch, deliver us, we beseech thee, from the scourges of God. Through thy intercessions preserve our bodies from contagious diseases, and our souls from the contagion of sin. Obtain for us salubrious air; but, above all, purity of heart. Assist us to make good use of health, to bear suffering with patience, and after thy example to live in the practice of penitence and charity, that we may one day enjoy the happiness which thou hast merited by thy virtues.

St. Roch, pray for us.

St. Roch, pray for us.

St. Roch, pray for us.

There is testimony that many people, even Protestants, and men, have had wounds cured and been healed of diseases by prayer in this chapel. To this distant shrine come ladies from all parts of the city to make the "novena" — the prayer of nine days, with the offer of the burning taper — and here daily resort hundreds to intercede for themselves or their friends. It is believed by the damsels of this district that if they offer prayer daily in this chapel they will have a husband within the year, and one may see kneeling here every evening these trustful devotees to the welfare of the human race. I asked the colored woman who sold medals and leaflets and renewed the candles if she personally knew any persons who had been miraculously cured by prayer or novena in St. Roch. "Plenty, sir, plenty." And she related many instances, which were confirmed by votive offerings on the walls. "Why," said she, "there was a friend of mine who wanted a place, and could hear of none who made a novena here, and right away got a place, a good place, and" (conscious that she was making an astonishing statement about a New Orleans servant) "she kept it a whole year!"

"But one must come in the right spirit," I said.

"Ah, indeed. It needs to believe. You can't fool God."

One might make various studies of New Orleans; its commercial life; its methods, more or less antiquated, of doing business, and the leisure for talk that enters into it; its admirable charities and its medieval prisons; its romantic French and Spanish history, still lingering in the old houses and traits of family and street life; the city politics, which nobody can explain, and no other city need covet; its sanitary condition, which needs an intelligent despot with plenty of money and an ingenuity that can make water run uphill; its colored population — about a fourth of the city — with its distinct social grades, its superstition, nonchalant good-humor, turn for idling and basking in the sun, slowly awaking to a sense of thrift, chastity, truth-speaking, with many excellent order-loving, patriotic men and women, but a mass that needs moral training quite as much as the spelling-book before it can contribute to the vigor and prosperity of the city; its schools and recent libraries, and the developing literary and art taste which will sustain book-shops and picture-galleries; its cuisine, peculiar in its mingling of French and African skill, and determined largely by a market unexcelled in the quality of fish, game, and fruit — the fig alone would go far to reconcile one to four or five months of hot nights; the climatic influence in assimilating races meeting there from every region of the earth.

But whatever way we regard New Orleans, it is in its aspect, social tone, and character *sui generis*; its civilization differs widely from that of any other, and it remains one of the most interesting places in the republic. Of course social life in these days is much the same in all great cities in its observances, but that of New Orleans is markedly cordial, ingenuous, warm-hearted. I do not imagine that it could tolerate, as Boston does, absolute freedom of local opinion on all subjects, and undoubtedly it is sensitive to criticism; but I believe that it is literally true, as one of its citizens said, that it is still more sensitive to kindness.

The metropolis of the Southwest has geographical reasons for a great future. Louisiana is rich in alluvial soil, the capability of which has not yet been tested, except in some localities by skilful agriculture. But the prosperity of the city depends much upon local conditions. Science and energy can solve the problem of drainage, can convert all the territory between the city and Lake Pontchartrain into a veritable garden, surpassing in fertility the flat environs of the city of Mexico. And the steady development of common-school education, together with technical and industrial schools, will create a skill which will make New Orleans the industrial and manufacturing centre of that region.

The vendor of fowls pokes in his head at every open window with cries of "Chick-EN, Madamma, Chick-EN!" And the seller of "Lem-ONS — fine Lem-Ons!" follows in his footsteps. The peddlers of Ap-PULLS!" of "Straw-BARE-eries!" and "Black-brees!" — all own sonorous voices. There is a handsome Italian with a somewhat ferocious pair of black eyes who sells various oddities, and has adopted the word "lagniappe" for his war-cry — pronouncing it Italianwise.

He advances noiselessly to open windows and doors, plunges his blazing black glance into the interior, and suddenly queries in a deep bass, like a clap of thunder, "LAGNIAPPA, Madam-a! — La gniap-PA!" Then there is the Cantelope Man, whose cry is being imitated by all the children:

"Cantel-lope-ah!
Fresh and fine,
Jus from the vine,
Only a dime!"

There are also two peddlers, the precise meaning of whose cries we have never been able to determine. One shouts, or seems to should, "A-a-a-a-ah! SHE got." Just what "SHE got" we have not yet been able to determine; but we fancy it must be disagreeable, as the crier's rival always shouts — "I-I-I! — I want nothing!" with a tremendous emphasis on the I. There is another fellow who seems to shout something which is not exactly proper for modest ears to hear; but he is really only announcing that he has fine potatoes for sale. Then there is the Clothespole Man, whose musical, quavering cry is heard at the distance of miles on a clear day, "Clo-ho-ho-ho-ho-ho-h-ho-se-poles!" As a trilling tenor his is simply marvelous. The "Coaly-coaly" Man, a merry little Gascon, is too well known as a singer to need any criticism; but he is almost ubiquitous. There is also the fig-seller, who crieth in such a manner that his "Fresh figs!" seems to be "Ice crags!" And the fan-sellers, who intend to call, "Cheap fans!" but who really seem to yell "Jap-ans!" and "Chapped hands!" Then there is the seller of "Tow-wells" and the sellers of "Ochre-A" who appear to deal in but one first-class quality of paint, if we dare believe the mendacious sounds which reach our ears; neither must we forget the vendors of "Tome-ate-toes!" Whose toes? We should like to know.

from LAFCADIO HEARN,
"Voices of Dawn," *Daily City Item*,
July 22, 1881

I live in a low altitude triangle. A triangle that seems to be placed in an acoustically perfect location. Sounds, many and varied, are offered up to me simply for my enjoyment, like a dessert cart overloaded with sweets when you're already full from dinner. This triangle's repertoire includes screaming winds and jaw dropping lightning. I am gifted with more sounds in one day than I heard in any given year in the place where I lived before. I had often wondered if my own thoughts qualified as sounds. I found the answer.

Triangular Sound Bites

SAM JASPER

Just outside the French Quarter's down river side is a section of town called the Marigny Triangle. Parcelled out by the profligate son of a wealthy plantation owner to pay debts accrued by his wine, women, song and gambling, it was bought up piecemeal until the plantation was all gone. It became New Orleans' first suburb. It shaped itself into a literal triangle with the apex at the river, fanning out in a maze of winding streets, a web that even some locals get lost in.

Stealing a line from "Sweet Bird of Youth," "I had to go all the way to New Orleans for it! Like it?"

"Oh my," my thoughts answer, no longer wondering if they themselves are a sound. "Why yes sir, I do like it so very much. I can't thank you enough!" The voice of my thoughts has a slight tinge of a drawl in its more grateful, romantic moments.

Then my day of gluttony starts.

A train whistles close by, sometimes using a long then short code. The engine chugs, as engines are wont to do, in time with the wheels' chorus scraping and screeching along the tracks by the river. Sometimes it's just one show a week; sometimes the train will perform two shows a day. The one for the real night owls starts at four in the morning. If the engineer applies the brakes and puts the train into reverse, the sound becomes a mechanical freeform jazz piece. I smile into my pillow, listening, then go back to sleep wondering what that train is carrying and to whom. How many others along its route will appreciate its music?

A large container ship winds its way up the river a little past daylight. The ship's horn blasting baritone concertos, letting all smaller craft know that it's navigating the hairpin turn in the river at Algiers Point. I picture an avant-garde conductor, dressed in white tie and tails, standing on the Moonwalk, baton in hand, pointing to the container ship with gusto, then to a tug which answers in a higher tone. The conductor tosses his hair back and holds his breath as he points to the ferry, knowing that the cymbal clang of its ramps and short toot can only be heard if the wind is right. Today he is relieved. The composition is complete for his audience of one in the triangle, still in bed listening, wondering if there will be another movement played.

As the dog is let out in the morning, the back fence of the long yard starts booming like drums in a primeval forest, shaking the elephant ears and forcing the delicate jasmine to shudder. Behind the fence is a stable used for housing the mules that draw the carriages for tours around the Quarter. There are thirty mules waking up, kicking the backs of their stalls with the full force of their shod hooves. One, two, three, pause. I can feel them waiting, poking their long faces out over the chain drawn across the front of their lodgings. One, two, three, louder this time, making their impatience known to all and sundry. The backyard forest returns to serenity only after they've been fed, the mules' attention having now been turned to oats soaked in molasses, sweet feed to start the day.

A siren rips through the awakening streets, starting softly, getting louder and louder until it recedes into the distance. A police call, an ambulance or a fire truck? I can't identify the difference but say a silent prayer for whoever needed the help the siren is bringing.

Oh, today must be Tuesday. The farrier is shoeing the mules. The sharp sound of a hammer on metal comes through my walls intermittently as he goes from one to the next. The hammer's banging is usually interrupted by the ill-tempered stable overseer, a man who is gifted with a colorful linguistic style.

"You stupid mule, get in there. Raggedy ass mule! You're more full of shit than a brass monkey! Dodo boyd. Shoo-ee," he rants, often sprinkling various obscenities into his non-stop spoken-word tirade, successfully hiding the fact that he secretly considers the mules his best friends, definitely preferring them to humans. Now and then he'll toss a tool across the yard, and a metal-against-concrete skitter can be heard, followed by more cussing and carrying on, trying to insure his reputation as the meanest Creole the Lord ever put on this Earth. Most humans believe it. The mules know better.

After they've eaten and the day-shift mules have been hitched up to their carriages, the night-shift mules have a conversation. A combination of eerie, high-pitched Jacob-Marley-in-chains sound followed by a whinnying bray. They must be discussing the last night's tours like cabbies waiting at the airport.

"Yeah, Pete, I had this drunk guy from Mississippi who just kept hollering, but I had six loads, so it wasn't a bad night. Little old ladies don't tip much, my driver says. He was saying words after that third load that would have made my mama put her head in her oat bag up to her ears!"

"Oh, Buster, did ya hear those bad jokes your driver was telling? Ha, I don't know how you put up with it! And the arm waving he does as he goes past the Cabildo! What is THAT about? Hey, here comes Mr. Okra! Maybe my driver will buy me some carrots. Ya think?"

Just then a human voice, amplified and distorted through some kind of bullhorn arrangement interrupts them. The neighborhood dogs have been barking for a couple minutes now, but as the voice gets closer, they start to howl.

It is Mr. Okra. The mules were right. It must be about eleven in the morning.

Selling his vegetables and fruit from the back of his truck, the hood of which is decorated with a multitude of plastic veggies, the side hand lettered crookedly with MR. OKRA, he drives a grid, singing his song:

I have apples and bananas.
I have grapes and pears.
I have cantaloupe.
I have eggplant.
I have onions and peppers.
I have potatoes and yams.
I have carrots.
I have celery.

He can remember every bit of his inventory and sing a verse for each. The rhythm is always the same, carefully laid over years of singing it the same way. It's sort of a five, five, four, four, five, five beat as he cuts a syllable here or there to make it fit. The first two words are lower notes ascending slightly, the inventory words up two or three notes from there with a drop down on the last syllable. In this triangle, time can be told by his song and timelessness can be experienced through it. A hundred years ago another Mr. Okra probably sang the same song from a mule-driven cart rather than a truck with a loudspeaker. The song, no doubt, was similar. His rhythm is so invariable that I can dance to the front door to make my purchase and never miss a beat. I can hear him in my head even now, hours after he's passed, his song replacing my thoughts and convincing me again that thoughts do indeed have a sound, but this time it's his song.

Workmen on the house next door holler to each other about the location of the hammer, is the saw plugged in, occasionally cursing when something doesn't go right. Some days they'll have some music playing, but mostly they talk, call out for each other, laugh and pound the siding onto the house. Human voices coupled with the sound of industriousness. Sounds the Earth has heard over and over through centuries as her inhabitants build on her surface. Only the tools have changed.

It must be going on two. I can't believe it's afternoon already, but it must be. The calliope on the Natchez is already playing "You Are My Sunshine" to be followed by the player's usual repertoire of old standards and ersatz riverboat songs. I can't hear the water of the Mississippi churning through the red paddles, but if I close my eyes, I can see it. I can hear the calliope play until the old riverboat moves down the river with a hold full of tourists, and I know that in most other cities that sound would be out of place unless a circus was coming to town or an amusement park was being visited. Here, in my house, it is a gift that's never a surprise but welcome like the butterscotch candy Grandma always had in the jar on the table. Comforting, reliable, even down to the playlist. If the calliope is playing on the Natchez, then things are reasonably okay in New Orleans today, silly though that may sound.

Getting on toward three in the afternoon now. The Mc-Donough 35 marching band is practicing again. They practice every day, even weekends as Mardi Gras approaches. Cold weather or rain never deter them. I can hear them from my desk chair, getting better and tighter. The sound carries the six or so blocks from the high school to my house with such clarity that some days I believe they will march right down my hall in full dress uniforms, brass sparkling, drums pounding, feet in perfect time. Oops, someone screwed something up. The music stops. The music director no doubt correcting someone and reminding them that they have only one more week 'til they're marching down St. Charles with thousands listening to them. The music starts again. This time they finish the song. Not one mistake. I'm proud of them, sitting warm in my office on a gray, cold day but they'll never know until I scream out, "Go Mc 35!" from behind a police barricade during a parade.

The day-shift mules come clopping back; their work is done. Soon the night-shift mules won't have time to talk.

Church bells are ringing. Each peal lingering in the air for a while, carrying it to my house just before the next strike of the bell. The bells come from different directions, so I'm never sure if they belong to St. Augustine's or St. Louis Cathedral, although the Cathedral's bells, like the ferry horn, can only be heard properly if the wind is right. I wonder if the bells are calling people to services, or is it a wedding? No it's not Saturday yet, I don't think. Maybe a funeral, but in this place the solemnity of the bells will shortly be followed by the unmistakable brass band dirge of a second line. I am lulled into inactivity by both the bells and the brass band as I hear life and death in the music.

Some Sundays, if I'm lucky I'll hear a kick up your heels second line coming down to Rampart from St. Claude. Beer bottles being hit with sticks to keep time, high-pitched whistles tweeting and an indefinable sound that follows it. It is the sound of people dancing, laughing, hooting, children excitedly chasing each other down the block trying to catch up and join in. It is the sound of joy. It bangs on my door and shouts, "Hey, *you*, you're here, you're alive, you ain't doing nothing to speak of, so *c'mon*. Dance!"

It really must be getting late now.

The clip clop of the mules coming home joined by a "Get up, mule!" comes past the house. It's the first of many carriages at this time of night. I count. One, two … five, six, seven. Must have been a big night for there to be that many. Some of the mules trot past, hurrying home to their dinner. Others, tired from their day, plod slowly and determinedly, the driver just along for the ride. Both ready to be done.

It's about eleven o'clock. This feast was just what was served up as I sat in my house. This triangle's hunger for sound is never sated. Nor is mine. The music of this city in all its forms inhabits me.

If I leave the house right now I can probably catch the Soul Rebels over on Frenchman; they'd be just about starting now. But once there I might get yanked into the Apple Barrel by some musicians I've not seen before, and wait, what's coming out of *that* door over there?

It's been a long day. I'm bloated from my feast. I won't go out tonight. I'll get in bed and wait for the train's nightly show and hope that tomorrow a second line will bang on my door, tugging me out, seducing me with sound.

"Hey, you can hear the music from your house, but if you come with me, you can hear the human voices. You can live today. You can dance today. *C'mon!* You ain't doing nothing to speak of."

And I'll go. Because this triangular piece of earth wants to nurture me with sounds. I have chosen this triangle. I can survive here.

I'll no doubt become spoiled rotten by the generosity of this place. Although crippled by a hurricane, it gives what it can, and that's still head and shoulders above most other places. The least I can do is accept the gifts I'm offered, so as not to offend.

Once in a bar, I asked my friends a question: "If God came down and told you you had two choices. Two only. First choice: Live ten more years here with the feast of sound, then die. Second choice: Live forty more years elsewhere without it, then die. What would you choose?"

Only one person out of eight chose those extra years.

It wasn't me.

"I think NOCCA [New Orleans Center for Creative Arts] in that time, in your time, will be looked back on like the Hudson painters of New York and the impressionists of France at the turn of the century. I'm serious about this. I see you smiling. And he didn't give me this folks. I'm serious. I think they're gonna look back on this time and realize that it was a resurgence of American music, and Ellis Marsalis will be revered for teaching this group of young men and women the importance of the music and giving them this platform to go and really change how the music was seen in the world at that time.

I remember, when I was in school, Wynton and Branford and Donald and Terence, all those guys thought they were going to New York just to become music teachers. Because that's how the music was 'sick,' I like to say ... people weren't supporting it, especially here in New Orleans, the way it should be. And then they went to New York, and they saw that there was a viable scene, and then they were the young lions that kind of did this whole resurgence."

Wendell Pierce, March 16, 2009, on "The Life and Times of Irvin Mayfield," WGSO, 990 AM

When Terence Blanchard strolled down a destroyed street playing his trumpet, past piles of debris, shattered houses, shattered lives, he began to transform that pain into art. He came as close as one can get to taking those ruins of New Orleans and directly changing it all into beauty, an eloquent expression of that pain. Such a moment, captured in Spike Lee's documentary *When the Levees Broke (A Requiem in Four Acts)*, does not make that pain disappear, of course; it does, however, show something about the spirit of the city.

On Terence Blanchard

DAVID RUTLEDGE

In addition to the dirge that he played on that destroyed street, Blanchard has done what he can to bring New Orleans back to life. He was integral in bringing the Thelonious Monk Institute of Jazz to Loyola University New Orleans in August 2007. According to a *Times-Picayune* article in April of that year, "The idea [for the Monk Institute] to leave Los Angeles came last fall from Blanchard, who said he had been wanting to do something to spur his hometown's recovery." What better way to rebuild the real New Orleans than to bring jazz to the city? This is the kind of thing that our city needs in order to keep its soul, and its soul truly is threatened in this post-Katrina era. In regard to some other cities that were interesting in hosting the institute, Blanchard said, "Those people just don't love this music the way we do. They don't have a history the way we do ... So my first reaction was, why go to those places? Bring the music to New Orleans."

Blanchard has been bringing music to this city for some time. His is a great New Orleans success story — someone untainted by politicians, unbroken by Katrina. The story of Terence Blanchard is the kind of story New Orleans needs right now. It is a story not only of a traditional New Orleans culture, but of a resilient culture. One that cannot only resist the forces that threaten it, but thrive.

THE STORY OF HIS MUSIC begins early. He began playing piano when he was five, under the watchful eye of his father. After hearing Alvin Alcorn play some traditional New Orleans jazz in elementary school, he decided to turn to the trumpet. At the same time, he says that his father had just gotten a piano: "It was an interesting day in our house." In high school he attended the New Orleans Center for Creative Arts, where his teachers included Ellis Marsalis and Roger Dickerson. He then earned a music scholarship and left New Orleans for Rutgers University in New Jersey.

His musical education intensified when he dropped out of college in 1982, replacing Wynton Marsalis in Art Blakey's Jazz Messengers. "My father had a problem with this for many years," he says in an interview with Terry Gross. In that same interview he refers to Blakey's band as "the school of Art Blakey." The shadow of this group casts all the way back to the 1950s, and includes such famous names as both Wynton and Branford Marsalis, Freddie Hubbard, Wayne Shorter, Horace Silver, Curtis Fuller. Here Blanchard was a teenager, one of the "young lions," trying to find his voice and keep that luminary shadow out of his mind.

The process of finding his musical voice — of finding out who he is as a player — comes up often when Mr. Blanchard discusses his formative years. Speaking at Boston's Berklee College of Music, he explains the lesson that Art Blakey gave to his young trumpeter: "We were backstage and he said, '[Forget] Diz, [forget] Miles, Freddy, Woody, Clifford ... You're here to be yourself and the best musician you can be.' He told me that when I was nineteen years old, and I was scared to death." Similarly, Blanchard says that the New Orleans clarinetist Alvin Batiste gave him this advice: "The easiest thing in the world is to play like John Coltrane. The hardest is to play like yourself."

Of course, the grand shadow of Miles Davis, the creator of so many innovative styles, can intimidate any upcoming trumpet player. Blanchard also describes his process of self-discovery as the process of understanding that he could not be his idol. He told the Berklee crowd about meeting Miles backstage: "The thing I realized right away was that I could never be him because I looked at his personality. I looked at him as a man and knew we were two different people. Then I was scared because this is my hero, this is the guy I'm trying to emulate. I wondered, 'What's next?'" He also relates Miles' words of encouragement to him: "Keep playing, motherfucker. Keep doin' whatcha doin'!"

The confidence and education that he gained in the Jazz Messengers led Blanchard to move on and form his own style. As Curtis Fuller puts it, "When Terence came into the band he was timid like I was, but he came out a monster." He first began forging his style in a band with fellow New Orleanian Donald Harrison, then, beginning in 1990, in his own group. He moved back to New Orleans in 1995, where he further honed that personal style. In fact, while Blanchard's music cannot be easily categorized as "New Orleans music," this return home was very significant for the development of his style. "If you wanted to be in Art Blakey's band, you had to be a New Yorker," he says in one interview. Blanchard gained great experience by leaving New Orleans, and he continues to be influenced by music from around the world. Still, something about New Orleans is essential to putting that gumbo of influences together and making them work.

PERHAPS THE PERSONAL STYLE THAT he developed could be described as deceptive simplicity. Blanchard at his best has something of a streamlined style that avoids the electric noise of fusion or the dissonance of much experimental jazz. In a discussion of his 1992 CD *Simply Stated*, he describes his appreciation of Miles Davis' style in terms of simplicity: "Miles Davis always had the ability to play melodies in such a simply stated fashion ... yet be very poignant and profound." The same could be said of his own style, although he is certainly no imitator of Davis. Within simple notes, Blanchard can convey a depth of emotion.

This is not, of course, simple, and I can feel these written words hitting a limit while trying to describe this musical style. The words are necessarily inadequate. Other writers have also inadequately attempted to label Blanchard's style, to translate his notes into words. His style is often referred to as "post-bop." My favorite, though, is "post-phallic": one academic writes, "we might associate the rise of the post-phallic trumpet with a group of African-Americans who are more affluent, better-educated, and/or more class-conscious." Might. Might not. But I love the use of the word "rise" there.

Rather than search for descriptive words for the music, one would be better off listening. Check out *Wandering Moon* (2000), *Bounce* (2003), *Flow* (2005).

MUCH OF BLANCHARD'S FAME HAS come through his work with movie soundtracks. He is often associated with the films of Spike Lee. In fact, though, he has composed soundtracks for fifty-one films, thirteen of them by Lee. He has also contributed to nine other soundtracks. (Presumably, these numbers should all be preceded with "so far.") It was Spike Lee who gave Blanchard his first opportunity to score a film, as Blanchard explains in this undramatic depiction:

> I was working with Spike Lee on *Mo' Better Blues*, helping Denzel Washington with the technical aspects of portraying a trumpet player, and Spike heard me playing some of my own music at the piano. Later on, he asked me to score *Jungle Fever*, and that was the beginning of my film career.

Apparently the song Blanchard was playing on the piano — the song that launched his film career — is the beautiful "Sing Soweto."

Strangely, some have written about Blanchard's film work as though it is something that gets in the way of his creative production, as though this music is not as significant as his work on his jazz CDs. Jazzreview.com refers to his film work as "a lucrative second career" and states, "Fortunately, Blanchard has not neglected his own playing," as though his soundtracks are not "his own." Another site states that he has "developed a secondary career scoring features." That almost makes it sound as though the process is just filling in the music for a film, rather than composing unique music in its own right.

In fact, the art of scoring films has expanded Blanchard's musical thoughts in incalculable ways. Jazz is Blanchard's great passion: "When I stood next to Sonny Rollins at Carnegie Hall [on a gig in 1993] and listened to him play, that was *it* for me. I didn't give a damn if I ever wrote another film in my life." Although jazz may be *it,* having the opportunities to create film scores has pushed him in different creative directions that he would not have encountered as a jazz musician, or as he puts it, "I really enjoy writing film scores because it's a separate thing away from jazz. It's a different outlet for creative expression without pimping myself."

Blanchard's CD *Jazz in Film* is a strong counter-argument against anyone who thinks that scoring the music for a movie is somehow a creative "second." Here Blanchard teams up with Joe Henderson and re-teams up with Donald Harrison to play some of the great jazz tunes from movies such as *A Street Car Named Desire, Anatomy of a Murder* and *Taxi Driver.* He ends this excellent CD with one of his own tunes from Spike Lee's *Clockers.* If there are any jazz purists — or snobs — who feel that film work is somehow unworthy of a true musician, this collection should quiet them down. One might also look to a recent exhibit at MOMA called "Jazz Score," which featured some of the films on Blanchard's CD as well as movies such as *Shadows,* directed by John Cassavetes with a soundtrack by Charles Mingus, and *Jack Johnson,* with a soundtrack by Miles Davis. Blanchard, in his film work, is clearly aware of this history and his place within it.

The art of scoring a film is not only writing the music, but writing music that will help to tell a story. One reviewer (tracksounds.com) writes that Blanchard's score for *The Caveman's Valentine* helps to develop a sense of the main character:

> Terence Blanchard won't be accused of copying anyone
> else with this effort. While it is uniquely evocative at
> times, the overall feeling of the score, as the film dictates,
> is foreboding — a feeling most aren't looking to conjure

up through their musical experience. Those who happened to be thrilled by music of a darker nature may find this a worthwhile soundtrack to invest in.

David Sterritt, writing for *The Christian Science Monitor*, explains that the music for *Malcolm X* changes as the mood of the story changes: "Praise also goes ... to composer Terence Blanchard, whose music score darkens along with the mood of the story and the colors of the production design." Andrew Granade (soundtrack.net) describes one song from Spike Lee's film 25th *Hour*:

> Without a doubt ... the score's most powerful cue is the eighth, "Ground Zero." Blanchard has created a musical portrait of the events of September 11th and their aftermath with Cheb Mami's Arabic-flavored vocals standing in for the terrorists of al-Qaeda and Northumbrian pipes representing the New York Fire and Police Departments. After an initial outburst of these vocals and pipes, the cue diminishes to a subdued statement of the relentlessly sorrowful string theme. This level is maintained until in the last minute when a crescendo builds to a series of snare drum hits that shoot right into your gut. The energy then continues to build with the two elements of vocals and pipes waging a sonic battle backed by dissonant string and brass clusters until it all simply stops, the pipes dying away with nothing resolved. Obvious and manipulative? On paper, yes, but in execution handled perfectly.

I won't go through all fifty-one soundtracks. There are plenty of examples to show that Blanchard's work with film has expanded, rather than diminished, his artistic production. "I love films that make me question how I should approach them, it makes me think differently and pose some fundamental questions about writing music," Blanchard told the *Philadelphia Daily News*.

Film work has not only helped to expand Blanchard's palette; this work — which has brought with it a great deal of experience with orchestral arrangements — has also led to his magnificent *A Tale of God's Will (A Requiem for Katrina)*. More on that in a moment.

These points about the quality of Blanchard's cinematic music beg the question of whether or not the music holds up on its own, as one listens to it apart from the films. When removed from their cinematic context, does this music bear repeated listening? Any answer, of course, will be a matter of opinion. My own opinion is that some of the tracks certainly do, although it may not be easy to listen to the entirety of any given score. There is a tendency toward swelling strings and some cinematic melodrama. At other times, songs that may risk melodrama are able to achieve some true intensity. A good example of this is "Ground Zero," described earlier. And Blanchard clearly knows that a film score may not be the same as a work that one will listen to again and again: he reworked the score for *Malcolm X* and turned it into the fine *Malcolm X Jazz Suite*. There the strings are eliminated, although some of the epic sense is lost. Combining the two — the epic orchestral sense and the more intimate jazz sound — would be part of the greatness of *Requiem* fourteen years later.

One might ask how all of this relates to New Orleans music. Blanchard's approach goes against the idea that New Orleans music is finite and ready to be placed in a museum. New Orleans music does not merely need to be preserved; it needs to evolve. He writes that his role models in New Orleans music "though steeped in tradition, were free thinkers. So I understood that this music has to evolve, that it wasn't a stagnant art form." The influence of his hometown may come up in unexpected places. I hear the sound of New Orleans brass bands in the song "Fruit of Islam" on the *Malcolm X* score, for example. With Terence Blanchard at work, the definition of New Orleans music continues to change, as does the city.

THIS BRINGS US TO THE crowning achievement of Blanchard's career (so far), *A Tale of God's Will (A Requiem for Katrina)*. Here Blanchard combines his talent as a composer for orchestra with his brilliance as a performer in smaller jazz groups. Here there is no doubt that what he has adapted from the music he wrote for Spike Lee's documentary holds up on repeated listening. He has combined the dramatic touches of orchestra with the personal touches of trumpet, piano, saxophone, bass and drum.

Blanchard's response to Katrina has itself been something of a personal triumph. He first evacuated to Atlanta with his family, then found his way to Los Angeles where he was working on the soundtrack for Spike Lee's *Inside Man*. Lee informed him that he planned to make a documentary in response to the situation in New Orleans, and Blanchard's path toward *A Tale of God's Will* began.

Like so many New Orleanians, he returned to the city after having watched enough CNN to numb the average adult. There was an almost surreal disconnect in watching one's home destroyed through the lens of a national news show. The reality of that destruction was gut wrenching yet disturbingly distant. The repeated images were like some kind of emotional torture for the citizens of this city. No one who lived through those weeks will ever be quite the same. Of course, CNN and all the other news programs eventually found something more interesting to focus on, better and fresher pictures to entertain their audience. American media seems incapable of dealing with long-term stories.

It took a director like Spike Lee to come in and fill the gap where the so-called news left off. In his documentary, he gives voice to many who were all-but-voiceless through the disaster and its aftermath. He offers respect to those who had been disrespected, even placing their faces in appropriate frames. Perhaps the most poignant moment in the over four-hour film is the moment when Terence Blanchard returns with his mother to her flooded home.

On the introductory page of Blanchard's website (terenceblanchard.com) there is a description of this moment that reads like a poem. I would like to present it as one:

The room is damp.
The furniture is re-arranged.
The mold.
My mother is crying.
I am trying not to.
I am telling her that these are just things,
… things that can be rebuilt, or repaired, or rebought.
I know this is not true.
Nothing will be as it was.
Yes. Still …
And this moment needs to be seen by us,
the New Orleanians exiled in Houston …
… and Portland and Kalamazoo …
who will one day return and see their own homes …
and cry their own tears
just as we have seen and cried ours.

This is about the house where Blanchard grew up, where he first played piano under his father's tutelage. After the scene, a tearful Blanchard says in the film, "It's like I can't go home."

If I were to slip into academic language here, I would refer to this scene as a synecdoche for the city of New Orleans. Instead, I will make that same point through Blanchard's words, from November 2007: "If you cried for my mom, multiply that cry by hundreds of thousands because she represents so many others who have gone through the same thing — who've suffered and yet still want to rebuild, to go home." This quotation continues, showing the dedication that Blanchard and his family have to New Orleans: "As for my mom, we have just about everything done to rebuild her home. She will be back in it by the time you read this."

It is this insistence on his city — on the future of his city — that defines Blanchard since the flood. During the first Jazz Fest after Katrina (2006), Blanchard told the crowd that he has been letting everyone in other cities know that New Orleans is coming back: "Goddamn right we're coming back, 'cause we don't like y'all food and we hate y'all music." He added, "I came home, I had a fried oyster and like to cried." And Blanchard's Jazz Fest performances since the flood have been powerful. In 2007 he joined saxophonist Pharoah Sanders on stage after performing his own set. In 2008 he showed up with the Louisiana Philharmonic Orchestra and played a full set of songs from *A Tale of God's Will*.

He also let the crowd know that the "God" in that title is one of "mystery," a God whose will we really cannot know. Blanchard does not have the same God as John Hagee, the man who stated that New Orleans was destroyed because there was going to be a gay pride parade. (By that logic, if one looks at the areas destroyed by the floods and the fact that the French Quarter was relatively unscathed, God would actually appear to hate working people.) We might also note that Blanchard's sense of God's role in this disaster does not prevent him from placing the appropriate blame on people. In Lee's documentary, he states, "It pisses me off because it didn't have to happen."

With *A Tale of God's Will*, Blanchard has found a way to pursue his love for scoring films and his love for New Orleans. As *The New York Times* put it, "In some ways disaster prompted Mr. Blanchard to bring it all back home." This is not to suggest that any Terence Blanchard CD is a solo work. He has become the leader — the teacher — but he is distinctly a teacher who encourages his students to step up. This is another way in which Blanchard's skill as a musician has developed. This epic work includes pieces by each member of his group. "Mantra" is by drummer Kendrick Scott; "Ashé" is by pianist Aaron Parks. Working in his jazz groups allows Blanchard to put aside his role as orchestral leader, the role he must play when scoring a film; in these smaller groups he can encourage the other players to discover their voices. A guitarist from Benin and from a previous version of Blanchard's band, Lionel Loueke, came out with his own CD in 2008 entitled *Karibou*. Blanchard now plays the role that Blakey played earlier in his career, cultivating the "young lions."

Like most of Blanchard's work, his *Tale of God's Will* would not be classifiable as standard "New Orleans music." This one, however, is all about New Orleans. It speaks profoundly of the flood and the destruction. Blanchard describes the song "Levees": "The strings are the water; my trumpet, the cry for help that got no response for days." He brings the music home, and finds a way to move forward after the disaster. The word that Blanchard most often uses when describing *A Tale of God's Will* is "universal": "I didn't want to write New Orleans-style music — I wanted to write music that was more universal ... Because in my mind, this was a universal story of tragedy, hope, despair."

Of course, it is the particular — New Orleans — which led to this universal, and Blanchard is able to capture both levels. He is able to view the tragedy of New Orleans on a higher spiritual level — as the mystery of God's will — and at the local, practical level — rebuilding a home and stating, in Spike Lee's documentary, "Somebody needs to go to jail because those levees were never really maintained the way they should have been." There may be a level on which all that happened was God's will, and perhaps music is the best means for expressing that level, but there is another level on which the Army Corps of Engineers should be held criminally responsible. The two levels are not contradictory. We may want some lawsuits, but we also need our music. Through music, Blanchard is able create something that can help people feel the tragedy and take a step forward toward healing.

THAT DIRGE FROM *When the Levees Broke*, Blanchard playing "A Closer Walk with Thee," slowly walking through the ruined neighborhood where he had grown up, playing a melody in the midst of disaster — that dirge represents the first graceful steps up from the destruction of New Orleans. There Blanchard plays alone; it seems to be a personal dirge, while at the same time the traditional song speaks for the city. He took that same mood of grace and resilience and developed it into his requiem, *A Tale of God's Will*. This music is necessary for the city — for its healing, for whatever hope there is that the city can still be saved. The creation of something new in the aftermath of tragedy is the most hopeful statement one can make.

One might think of that moment as a permanent dirge, one that will echo forever through the streets of New Orleans.

Much background information for this piece comes from Anthony Magro's *Contemporary Cat: Terence Blanchard with Special Guests.* Other information comes from Blanchard's website, www.terenceblanchard.com. The other sources and links will be posted at www.chinmusicpress.com.

M

I am in New Orleans and I am trying to proclaim something I have found here and that I think America wants and needs.

There is something left in this people here that makes them like one another, that leads to constant outbursts of the spirit of play, that keeps them from being too confoundedly serious about death and the ballot and reform and other less important things in life.

The newer New Orleans has no doubt been caught up by the passions of our other American cities. Outside the "Vieux Carré" there is no doubt a good deal of the usual pushing and shoving so characteristic of American civilization. The newer New Orleans begs factories to come here from other cities. I remember to have seen page advertisements, pleading with factory owners of the North to bring their dirt and their noise down here, in the pages of the *Saturday Evening Post*, if I remember correctly.

However, I am sure these people do not really mean it. There are too many elements here pulling in another direction, and an older and I believe more cultural and sensible direction.

At any rate there is the fact of the "Vieux Carré" — the physical fact. The beautiful old town still exists. Just why it isn't the winter home of every sensitive artist in American, who can raise money enough to get here, I do not know.

SHERWOOD ANDERSON,
"New Orleans, the *Double Dealer*, and the Modern Movement in America" (1922)

New Orleans may be too seductive for a
writer. Known hereabouts as the Big Easy,
it may be too easy, too pleasant. Faulkner
was charmed to a standstill and didn't really
get going until he returned to Mississippi
and invented his county. The occupational
hazard of the writer in New Orleans is a
variety of the French flu, which might also
be called the Vieux Carré syndrome …

On the other hand, it is often a good idea
to go against the demographic trends,
reverse the flight to the country, return
to the ruined heart of the city. When the
French Quarter is completely ruined by the
tourists — and deserted by them — it will
again be a good place to live.

WALKER PERCY,
"Why I Live Where I Live,"
1980

The *Vieux Carré* is most beautiful in the early evening, when the subtle colors of a sunset provide a perfect complement to the concrete, creating a harmony of architecture on each street. An orange cloud strokes the sky with the exact shade as that balcony on the corner or of the dusk-colored brick wall that one happens to be passing. One treads lightly, at this hour, as though strolling through something delicate. Even the sidewalks seem softer. Degas, or some soul of lesser expression, may once have walked along these streets.

Asides on the Tuba

a short story by REX NOONE

Thoughts also have a softer tone during these evenings. So I chose this time to walk and think after a personally oppressive day. A day when my mind needed the relief of a pastel cityscape. The setting sun would cast intricate patterns through balcony railings, sending elaborate shadows across buildings, across walls. When the sun sets in the French Quarter, one can always feel the stirrings of some new life, as if each night is a time of unlimited potential.

Either the shadows were gaining strength, that evening, or the people were fading, becoming less colorful. Down the next street one heard the sound of tubas coming from a brief line of figures obscured by the shadows. As the final rays of the sunset sometimes flickered along the street, a face would become momentarily visible, the ghost of a nose, or a big horn would sometimes push out of the darkness, flashing a last brass gleam of the day's fading sunlight.

The deep sounds that came from these great horns were heavy with eloquence. Expressing the otherwise inexpressible. Conveying a personal weight which could flow only from the men with the heavier bellies. The men of the tuba. Something of the shadows themselves was expressed by those lowing horns, those lovingly blowing horns.

Quietly I pondered, reverently, while strolling past the shadows of these magnificent instruments.

The tuba deserves such reverence, such respect. Permit me to present a bit of its history. According to *The World Encyclopedia of Tuba History*, the word "tuba" derives from the Latin word for "tube," which is completely unfair. A tuba is no more or less a mere "tube" than, say, a saxophone, a clarinet or — that most offensive of woodwinds — the *oboe*. This word, of course, "oboe," derives from a Franco-Germanic conglomerate which roughly works out to "high wood." Oh boy. I know one such high-cultured *haut* boy myself, one who carries his horn where it is not needed and not wanted. Excuse me. Please disregard this digression. My personal disdain for the oboe is a topic that will need to be addressed elsewhere. My point here is only that the tuba has been disrespected for too long. The first tuba on record, that is, historical record, the first tuba verified by historians and archaeologists, goes back to the ancient Pharaohs. That is completely untrue, and I apologize.

Allow me to start my scales again, in another key. The following is true: my first lessons on this initially unwieldy instrument took place in the city of New Orleans when I was eight years of age. Being a slightly underdeveloped boy at that time (only to fill out gracefully and impressively in my late teens and early twenties), my first attempts on the tuba were nearly fatal. Forcing all of my lungpower into the instrument resulted in little more than a mockingly windy sound, a windy trickle from that wide brass orifice, that wide opening that seemed to hold so much promise, so much hope. A weak whisper of breath was all my entire body could express through that potentially opulent opening, and I nearly toppled to the floor with that brass weight wrapped over my torso.

Despite these difficulties, I persevered; I persevered, despite my first teacher stating that I was built for the flute. He thought that he knew the music merely because he was a distant cousin of some obscure Marsalis.

Gradually, this torso would grow into the instrument for which it lives, for which it was born. The tuba eventually ceased to be a great beast with which I was wrestling, and to whom I was usually losing, and came to be a unique companion, a solace. At times, during my adolescent years, the tuba became my sole means of self-expression. Luckily, in New Orleans, this instrument is not relegated to pep squad football bands. I found plenty of opportunities to practice with brass bands, jazz bands, such as the famous group The Mood Swings, and all sorts of people who were passionately attempting to discover and express their personal music.

Some, like myself, were attempting to translate the heavens through a tube.

The tuba is capable of abrupt turns and unpredictable flights. Sometimes I don't know what notes to expect from it.

There are women who will listen with commensurate respect to the efforts of an aspiring tuba player. Yes, there are. One who would sit and listen almost rapturously as I blew that tuba toward the highest realms. (Yes, toward the highest realms, although I will admit that I often only reach the ceiling.) It will not be trumpets that will sound at the gates of my heaven: it will be tubas. She knew that. Many times she was near tears. She would tell me that my playing was very good indeed. Even when she wanted to watch a favorite nightly game show or listen to some other type of music. That is very, very good, she would say. She would even buy new music for us to listen to, together, all the time, in fact, new music, so that we could listen to new possibilities for my Art.

Yes, she would, pal. Very, very good, she would say.

As I continue to stroll, along with these thoughts, recalling better days, the clouds begin to relinquish the light, but one — just above — still stubbornly holds to a bold orange.

The best music that I have produced has been with The Mood Swings. This was a group with whom I could truly work. The percussionist of this group tended to toy with silence, stopping on a heartbeat — forcing one to listen to what she called "the intervals of systole" — and reclusively moving from humor to blues. The bass player was constant yet creative and could challenge each of us in turn. We would feel the steady pace of that bass, then be surprised by the turquoise twist of its rhythm. A new truism, changing like a fact. Each of us adapting, responding. The piano player. I apologize. There was no piano player. Okay, I will admit that The Mood Swings were just a couple of friends of mine, but we did play quite well together at times. I cannot tell a lie. I will also admit that I have never been paid for playing the tuba. This was not intended to be a confession.

Let me return to the tuba: after extensive research, I have discovered that in three states it is technically illegal to drive a car while playing the tuba. Unfortunately, Louisiana is one of them. All I wanted was to take every possible opportunity to improve. It was a little awkward, squeezing behind the steering wheel, buckling in. But this created no hazard on the road. The judge's decision still seems like an insult. Keep your tuba where it belongs. It is not illegal to play certain other instruments while driving. That is clear discrimination. It also seems unfair that pointing this fact out for the judge should cause my fine to double. The tuba rarely receives its deserved respect. No one I know can name even a single tuba great.

There are only a few who understand my passion. Most of them are ghosts, shadowy figures on the periphery of the street.

Most people, for example, do not realize how versatile the tuba can be. When I offered this information to one person, a former friend, he said that, yes, it could be used as a giant planter. When she laughed at that, he said, or you could plug it up at one end and turn it into an ornamental pool, with lily pads and little frogs. When she laughed again, practically gasping for air, I left the room. An hour later, I thought of the perfect retort about an oboe, about a goddamn oboe.

The tuba *is* versatile. It has nothing to do with "oom-pah." That may be the first sound one makes when learning to play, but one does not judge the art of painting by beginner's strokes, one does not downgrade Picasso because others are only capable of fingerpaint. One does not dismiss literature because of kindergarten sentences. At its greatest, the tuba reaches ornithic brilliance. There are times when I have heard the tuba reach such levels of brilliance. I have heard it happen.

Okay, so I have not reached such heights myself. That doesn't explain anything. Few people appreciate that one may be profoundly inspired while being unable to express that inspiration convincingly. I am an inspired musician. I will purge these pages of all oom-pahs. It does not matter that I have been unable to find a band to play in. Yes, and I have a weight problem. Is that any reason to ostracize someone like a beast? Like some clunky and eccentric contraption that should be relegated to the margins?

The tuba parades. The tuba struts the gutter.

The tuba is partially fueled by fried foods. And I said some nasty things about vegetarians. How can she live on greens? There may have been some things, spoken by me, that I regret. From the gut, unthinkingly. Shouldn't one be given another chance? The oboe will solve nothing: it takes a tuba. I have very few real friends. I should erase that sentence. No. Who cares? I made up The Mood Swings. Is it all because I work as a waiter? Or worked. Tina, Tina. I need to concentrate.

Let me regroup.

Let me tell you something about the tuba. Everyone knows that Bill Clinton played one on TV before he was elected president. I considered that an act of bravery, and he earned my vote. But there is more. How many people know that John F. Kennedy regularly played a tuba to help him relax? That the sound of this instrument would often be heard coming from the oval office during such tension-filled moments as the Cuban missile crisis? How many people know that Abraham Lincoln wanted to give a brief tuba recital rather than deliver what he had written for his Gettysburg address? Later, he greatly regretted his failure to bring that instrument with him to offer a proper memorial for the Civil War dead.

How many people know that George Washington had to be persuaded to leave his tuba behind at the crossing of the Delaware? That he looked longingly back at his beloved brass as it settled into the snow, thinking of all those dedicated days of practice as he forged forward for the good of the country? The greatest sacrifice. It does not matter if any of this is true.

The tuba has a great and impressive reign through American history. It is not my fault that I was fired as a waiter for constantly knocking over co-workers and customers. As if they couldn't see me coming. That bananas Foster tragedy was purely an accident. It could have happened to anyone. The flaming tablecloth, the fire trucks that took too long because of French Quarter traffic. How can I be blamed for that? Customers should be careful what dessert they order when wearing loose clothing. Circumstance, bad luck. But I will not dwell on the negative.

As I walk alone, although perhaps not truly alone, through the streets of this *Vieux Carré*. I prefer the French name for this neighborhood, because the sounds of those two words can very nearly be expressed on the tuba, as if the instrument itself has an affinity for these streets.

My tuba waits for me, in a corner of my apartment, having gathered only a few days of dust. Perhaps by reaching this low point, I will be better constituted to pursue my Art. Perhaps my tuba will sing. It may be time to return to my room, possibly. To practice, to go on.

Almost all of the light has left from those previously impressive clouds, taking away their intensity, and that one orange cloud overhead, the one which had been holding so closely to its color, has faded to the dusted brick shade of this wall. Evening always alters, has its transition, and these passionate shadows gradually change to tangible night. This is only an interval.

These bricks, at night, illuminated by limited gaslights, rarely have a harmony. They hold only an indistinct rhythm. As if awaiting the day.

While the ghosts still serenade my walk. The ghosts of those few who were attuned. Those few who were truly attuned to the potential of this nearly anonymous instrument. They still serenade my walk, along with the countless walks of others, those who have pursued similar passions, artists to the heart, dedicated to a single sound, hoping for the appropriate note.

"Charbroiled oysters, fried oysters, oysters Rockefeller, oysters Bienville, po'boy sandwiches, shrimp Creole, shrimp tasso, fried shrimp, meat pies, red beans and rice, jambalaya, turtle soup, gumbo, anything fried or blackened."

Drew Brees, in response to Jay Leno asking him to name as many New Orleans foods as possible in 15 seconds, on the "*The Jay Leno Show*, " December 9, 2009

Though I had been to The Hill many times while living in St. Louis, I had never noticed the red, green and white fire hydrants dotting the neighborhood — all of them striped like squat, Italian-colored barber shop poles. It was a bright Saturday, and the sputtering of lawnmowers echoed through the streets, grooming the lawns of the modest brick bungalows, crowded duplexes and bocce gardens I knew so well after living in St. Louis for three years. I passed Mama Campisi's and all the other familiar pizzerias, delis and bakeries with names like Zia's and Amighetti's — a Little Italy surrounded by a city of rolling Midwesternness.

When We Make a Feast: Food as Prayer at the New Orleans Table

REGGIE J. POCHÉ

Yogi Berra played in these streets as a boy. And he may have attended St. Ambrose Catholic Church and its adjacent school (in the heart of The Hill), the place I had intended to be on that Saturday morning. A friend had told me that parishioners of St. Ambrose hold a St. Joseph Altar on the weekend nearest March 19, the feast day of the saint, the foster father of Jesus, and they invite the public to dine with them. It was a Sicilian festival tradition I had grown up with back home in Louisiana, where dozens of public and private altars of symbolic food dot the New Orleans metropolitan region every year. I never thought I'd find it elsewhere. Nearly seven months since Hurricane Katrina and the failure of the federal levees flooded the city, I still ached for home and hoped to find a little piece of it flung upriver in Missouri — at least a plate of altar spaghetti. But when I arrived at St. Ambrose, with its red brickwork and terra cotta of solemn Romanesque arches, I thought, *This just will not do.* Some hungers cannot be satisfied by substitution. They may have had spaghetti with a good tomato sauce, but definitely not with "red gravy" — a New Orleans term for spaghetti sauce. There could have been some nice store-bought salmon, but most certainly no Louisiana redfish. I turned around, moved northward on Kingshighway, and headed for my apartment.

There, I pulled a box from my closet, which had been undisturbed since I moved to St. Louis, and I found the touchstone I had been looking for — a videocassette transfer of a grainy Super 8mm film labeled "Altar, 1968." While growing up, I had frequently seen this film, among dozens of others, from the original Super 8 reel, but this was the first time I had watched it alone and away from home. None of my brothers were there to crowd around the canvas screen with me. No mother operating the projector at the back of the den. No flickering light, nor the constant clicking of the projector or the smell of dust burning on its hot bulb. But still, there's something about those old films, especially their silence — the absence of conversation, music and laughter — that spellbinds me. In its brief sixty seconds, the altar film showed me what I really longed to experience: the sense memory of fragrant olives and fried eggplant, a pleasant muddle of anise-perfumed bread and spaghetti with the obligatory "red gravy."

The film began with a view of the large front parlor of my great-aunt Vita Monica's Garyville home (about twenty-five miles upriver of New Orleans) in which the altar took up nearly every square foot. As on every altar I experienced as a child and teenager, and according to Sicilian custom, a statue of St. Joseph holding the infant Jesus stood above a wide lower table, atop a three-tiered, stepped platform — the number of which represents the Holy Trinity. The larger, lower table contained many of the symbolic breads, pastries and other traditional Sicilian delicacies found on any typical New Orleans altar.

I saw the mounds of colorful biscotti and sugar-dusted cannoli I coveted as a boy and laughed when I recalled my childish repulsion at the whole baked redfish that was always placed, front and center, on the table — its green olive eye staring back through a pupil of bright red pimento. Just as I had years ago, I delighted in seeing the cakes shaped like lambs covered in fleece of shaved coconut and the breads shaped like hammers, saws and other tools of the carpenter's trade. They were accompanied by bowls of *mudrica* — sweetened breadcrumbs representing sawdust — which is sprinkled over spaghetti in lieu of Parmesan cheese. Then there were the holy statues, most notably the head of Saint Mother Cabrini in her black nun's habit and with eerie glass eyes that would follow you around a room; her body had been claimed by Hurricane Betsy three years before. Amid the fruit baskets, the lacy fig cakes, the fried potato balls and the two dramatically long chianti bottles cradled in straw *fiaschi*, greenery of Japanese plum, bridal wreath, ivy and azalea and camellia blossoms sprouted where food hadn't been placed — all of it lit by candles and blessed by a priest. As a boy, I never thought to ask why I and so many others around New Orleans enjoyed such a feast annually. Here, ritual feasts, both secular and religious, abound. But still, why break bread in this way?

Oral legend holds that a severe drought and famine devastated Sicily in the Middle Ages. Crops died. Families starved. Only the hearty fava bean sustained a few. The faithful prayed for the intercession of St. Joseph to deliver them with rain, and once it fell, they knew their prayers had been heard. In gratitude for the island's survival, the people of Sicily, followed by their descendants in Louisiana, vowed to give thanks every March 19 by creating elaborate altars of food for display and distribution to the poor or any who are hungry, a festive ritual that became known as Tavola di San Giuseppe — St. Joseph's Table. I know it simply as The Altar, which was always comfortingly the same, year after year. I hadn't been born yet in 1968, but that film, my touchstone, could have been any altar — with many of the usual faces of family, friends and guests eating the same dishes.

I saw them when the film cut from Aunt V's parlor to the rest of the house where dozens of people were gathered — older women in hats smiling politely for the camera, younger ones, with teased hair, blinking through dark eye makeup, men with thin neckties smoking cigarettes, and the tops of boys' crew-cut heads darting through the bottom of the screen. Then they all flickered away.

And there was Aunt V, barely taller than those boys, directing plates of spaghetti to the tables of hungry visitors crowded throughout the house. This was Aunt V's altar, a devotion she would keep, as would so many men and women in and around New Orleans, for decades to come. She gestured over to my grandmother, a beauty when in her prime, who was dancing while stirring a pot of red gravy. The camera panned down her red dress (one of her best, I'm sure) and caught the blue terry-cloth slippers on her feet just before flickering out.

A second later, my mother came into view briefly, my father behind the camera. Then he got into a few frames while she filmed. They were both about twenty years old, both smiling and laughing, mouths moving in silent conversation. This was a year before my older brother was born, eleven years before I (along with my two other triplet brothers) was born, and thirteen years before their divorce. They could have been talking about anything.

I also saw other faces I knew and some I didn't. I saw relatives who had died before I was born and divorced spouses I had never met. But no matter my acquaintance with the faces that flickered in and out before the film ended, these people had all been led to that sixty-second moment on March 19, 1968, by one man, Epifanio Navarra, my great-grandfather, whose story had been brought up during the countless Sunday dinners of my childhood. Men and women like him decided, generations ago, that we should be here, cradled by the river on a pillow of mud, and I like to think that they want us to stay here.

A nineteen-year-old Epifanio arrived in New Orleans in 1901 via a long-established trade route with Sicily. Ships carrying citrus, figs and olives had been arriving for decades, but this new human cargo, to which Epifanio, his brother, and their mother belonged, would flood the city, at one point arriving weekly, for the next twenty years. Upon setting foot in this new country, my great-grandfather would have been undoubtedly greeted by the familiar: fruit vendors peddling the produce of his homeland, dock workers speaking in his mother tongue. I have imagined him, fearful yet hopeful, unskilled and poor, gathered with hundreds of others on the Calliope or Press Street wharves. Thousands had shared this experience, settled in and made a lasting contribution to New Orleans' culture. They added a Mediterranean essence to the existing African, Caribbean and Creole mélange of this American City.

In the early Twentieth Century, a section of the French

Quarter was known as Little Palermo, where Sicilian immigrants maintained their customs, language and cuisine in a few square blocks of decrepit tenements. They were lured there by *padroni*, labor agents charged with finding strong backs to work on the Mississippi and on the sugar-cane plantations upriver. Epifanio eventually settled in Garyville, married, became a shoemaker and reared five daughters. Many like him eventually became small merchants and established groceries, confectionaries, cobbler shops and other enterprises. Some even became strawberry farmers in the parishes north of the city, above Lake Pontchartrain. But no matter how industrious, no matter how American, their successive generations became, Sicily's customs, especially her folkways and her foodways, remain. Through these ritual traditions, I have come to know my great-grandfather and his people, as if we were sitting at the same table to celebrate health, good fortune, even survival.

The altar is a tradition born, and continuously renewed, through privation and tragedy, yet it vigorously celebrates life and the solace and protection of community, a purpose similar to the second line parades of New Orleans jazz funerals. The first Sicilian arrivals to New Orleans left the cholera and poverty of their homeland behind for yellow fever, more poverty and a native population suspicious of this new group of foreigners. As prosperous Americans, they sent their first native-born generation off to two world wars and prayed to St. Joseph for a safe return. Later, they dedicated altars to casualties of Vietnam, then both Iraq wars. Food was consecrated after the Twin Towers had fallen and after two space shuttles had crashed and then again after Katrina had drowned thousands in our own city. Through all, the altars have been there to give us comfort.

Although the tradition had been imported to many

American cities — and they continue today in small Italian enclaves of Texas, Missouri, California and New York — nowhere have these altars remained as vital to cultural identity, to both Italian and non-Italian alike, than in New Orleans and its surrounding parishes, where an estimated 200,000 people are of Sicilian descent, the highest per capita population anywhere in the United States. Natives are wont to say that everyone here has at least one Italian grandmother, and these grandmothers are the ones who have kept this tradition alive.

Aunt V, Epifanio's second-eldest daughter, was one such grandmother. No matter how many altars I may experience in the future, no matter how many I've seen in and around New Orleans, none will ever be as sumptuous, as joyous, as Aunt V's. She had been taught the art by her mother-in-law, Philippa, who came to Louisiana from Salaparuta — a village near Epifanio's home of Contessa Entellina. It's easy for me to picture Vita as a young, seventeen-year-old wife, barely five feet tall and as eager to please Philippa as she was to laugh — decades before arthritic knees and a stroke stole her vigor but never her good humor and childlike mischievousness.

During my earlier childhood, it was tempting to steal some small trifle from her altar table, but, out of respect, I never did — except for maybe this one time. I couldn't have been more than seven years old, bug-eyed and dazzled by the jewel-colored *biscotti* placed about the table. But customarily, all visitors are forbidden to eat from (or "break") the altar until later in the day. I remember standing at the table with my mother and my brothers — her three little ducklings, she used to say.

"Say a prayer," she said, pulling us to her side.

I'm sure I obliged or at least looked penitent with folded hands. But what I do remember, clearly, is reaching for a shiny, green cookie, which I knew from experience would be mint flavored. My mother's firm hand grabbed me at the wrist, guided the cookie back to its place, while the other hand pinched me on the arm.

"Of course, you'd be the one to go and touch it," she reprimanded quietly.

Maybe I cried afterwards. I'm not certain. But it was enough to get Aunt V's attention. She hobbled over, calling to me, the strain on her knees ever-present in her voice.

"Come here, my darlin'," she said, laughing. It's her laugh that is easiest to remember. Even today, we all remember it: a sweetly chirping, softly lilting bit of a munchkin squeak. "Go see your Maw-Maw in the kitchen," she said.

I ran ahead, through the parlor, the dining room, past family, friends, the local "villagers" of Garyville, and she followed as fast as she could.

"Fran," she said to my grandmother, "give some cookies to the boys."

Always the dutiful little sister, even at sixty-nine, and a steadfast helper in preparing the altar for over forty years, my grandmother stopped filling plates with fried eggplant and went directly to the large Tupperware containers, as big as treasure chests, stacked on the landing of the kitchen stairs.

"For the boys," my grandmother said, and I got three little bags of cookies. But before I could go and enjoy the contraband with my brothers, Aunt V took the bags from my hands, opened up two, removed a green cookie apiece from each, and put them in my own bag.

"Extra two for my Regg," she giggled. "When you were a baby, you were mine. We would take you boys out somewhere, and your Maw-Maw had Ross, your mama had Rhett, and I had my Regg."

She would tell me this again and again, even as a teenager, when stealing sips of wine replaced my zest for St. Joseph cookies, and into adulthood, when my pleasure became sitting with a bowl of steamed altar artichokes drizzled with olive oil — a small slice of Romano cheese and a clove of garlic hidden in each leaf. The ritual of pulling out a leaf and scraping it through my clenched teeth to get the thin layer of tender flesh will always hold some fascination.

It is ritual, both secular and religious, that sustains us all. It strengthens us, shores us against life in this vulnerable, preposterous city — just as it had for past generations, those we honor on All Saints Day with freshly whitewashed tombs. We also speak their names over the communion of a crawfish boil, celebrate their lives, well-lived lives, in a second-line parade, and board up our homes and brace for the storms just as they had taught us.

In these rituals, a skeptic like me can find a sense of the holy and wonder at their power to remind us of who we are, where we've been and where we are going. The ritual foodways of the St. Joseph Altars, especially, give me this grace. A feast in the middle of Lent's austerity may seem like a contradiction to many, but they'd understand once they beheld a table of lobster and local red snapper dressed on silver platters and boiled shrimp and crawfish complimented with symbolic, blessed breads in the shape of the shepherd's staff, the Sacred Heart, the crucifix — a New Orleans miracle of loaves and fish for the multitudes. Delicate *cannoli*, cream puff *sfingi*, and *cuccidati* fig cookies sweeten our lives as much as Dixieland Jazz. *Pignolatti*, fried dough covered in caramelized sugar and shaped like pine cones, said to be Christ's only childhood toys, show us that our poverty cannot deny simple pleasures, especially our propensity for myth-making. *Pupacoulova*, brightly colored eggs nestled in their own bread pillows, remind us that death can renew and that our old creole-colored homes will survive future storms. *Mudrica*, those breadcrumbs representing the sawdust of Joseph's trade, instructs us that we do not toil in vain. Pasta Milanese, made of our beloved "red gravy," declares that food is our lifeblood and that we should keep our creative tongues. It's all magic baked in our ovens, simmered on our stoves. And in New Orleans, magic is passed around.

For a while, I carried a dried fava bean with me — a magical, blessed bean I received at the last of Aunt V's largest altars — before age robbed her of her strength to continue the tradition. It was 1999, and my brother and I would be traveling to France in three months. She wanted us to have a little protection, so she set two beans aside. Typically, along with a few cookies, some blessed bread and a prayer card, a bean is given to each altar visitor as a token of the day — a little lagniappe, as New Orleanians say. The beans are to remind us of the famine from which St. Joseph's intercession delivered the peasants of Sicily, and they are to keep us safe once again from poverty and hunger. It's not uncommon to find a bean among the change of a coin purse or tucked away in a pantry here. The bread is also kept for protection, the crumbs thrown into the wind of a gathering storm so that it may pass safely. I can only imagine how many times this ritual played itself out in the hours before Katrina made landfall or the thousands of lucky beans that were nervously thumbed during the television weather forecasts.

I once showed my own bean to Aunt V four years after it crossed the Atlantic with me. My grandmother had suffered a stroke the week before Easter, some months after Aunt V's own stroke — a later complication of which put them in the hospital at the same time. After leaving my grandmother's room to finish her evening rosary with her one "good hand," as she calls it, I moved three doors down and knocked at Aunt V's darkened room.

"My Regg," she said upon seeing me. I kissed her and took a seat next to the bed. Her eyes were swollen and red, and she blotted her cheeks with tissue. I had never before seen her without her eyeglasses. I asked if she had been crying because her children had just left for the evening. She said no. I thought that maybe she was in pain like before, but that wasn't it. "You'll probably be out of here in a couple of days," I said to reassure her.

"That's not it," she said. "Your Maw-Maw's missing her Holy Week. Why did she have to get a stroke, too?"

She changed the subject to ask me about my brothers and when I was going to move to St. Louis for graduate school.

"My mama was born in Missouri," she said. "A lot of Italians in Kansas City."

"I know," I replied. "Ya'll talk about Big Mama all the time."

"I wish you could have known her."

"But I do," I said, "because of all the stories ya'll tell. She was christened Anna Sagona, born in Kansas City, parents were Sicilian immigrants. And my grandma cooks spaghetti and meatballs every Sunday just like Big Mama taught her."

At this, she let out her little munchkin laugh. I felt comforted to know it was still there — after being widowed when her children were still very young, then after losing two adult sons to heart attacks — through years of debilitating knee pain and a final series of strokes. Through it all, she thought only of her God, her family and her altar. I showed her my old lucky bean, which I said would come with me to Missouri, where I was when she died six months later.

Certainly, scholars could rightly explain that the altars have remained so widespread here because of the sheer number of Sicilian immigrants like Epifanio, who came to this region and fathered generations. Maybe the fact that the Sicilians came to a city whose dominant religion was the same as their own had something to do with it. Even St. Joseph's feast day, March 19, coincides with the Mi-Carême celebration that had been popular with Louisiana's French-speaking Creoles. This mid-Lenten celebration broke the forty-day fast with a day of frivolity and indulgence. The Italians simply added to a party that had been going since Louisiana was a colony.

But ultimately, I believe that the Sicilians who made this city home gave us yet another graceful way to cope with our mortal lives — the hardship and loss of all men and women, but especially those of us in New Orleans. They have given us a touchstone with our past and another way to celebrate and share and pass the food around — a typically New Orleans impulse. It's a human impulse, a second line we all follow until the saints go marching in.

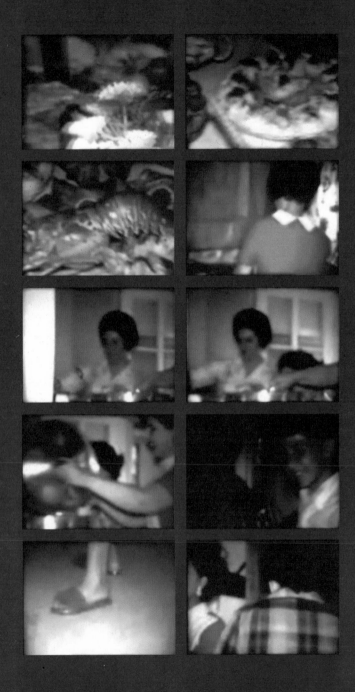

When I returned to New Orleans to attend university two years after Katrina, I noticed, being tattooed myself, all of the Katrina tattoos. Everyone had them: young, old, middle class, gutter punks, soccer moms. I realized how many people, unbeknownst to one another, had gone out and gotten these Katrina-inspired tattoos. In the beginning, I thought of the tattoos as a cathartic act, but the more time I spent on the project and the more people I interviewed, the more I realized that I was really dealing with what I would call a "Grace experience." The Jesuits have a great saying: "Find God in everything." I found that idea in these stories.

Tattooing Katrina

REBECCA FREELAND-HEBERT
Photography by Sandra Burshell

Grace has many faces and means different things to different people. For people who lived in New Orleans before and after the storm, Grace came to them through Hurricane Katrina. Some felt the hurricane was sent by God in a revelatory way; others felt God in a cooperative way, in their own actions and the actions of those around them, interacting with people, both positive and negative, good and evil. Grace is experienced during highs and lows. People who don't believe in God also had Grace experiences. For some, Katrina brought about an immense sense of pride in where they live,

and they wanted a permanent declaration. All the stories are different but they all have one thing in common: love. Love for their city, family, pets, strangers, God, themselves and New Orleans.

I began my project with an ad in the local free paper *Gambit Weekly*, offering thirty dollars cash and fresh baked goods. I was going to make cookies, but instead went with a friend's mother's recipe, "Frieda's Fancy." We don't know the real name of the recipe; we named it that after her mother had given it to me to sell in my café. Frieda was Dutch, and it is a simple war recipe of 1 egg, ½ a cup of butter, 2 cups of flour, 1 cup of sugar and sliced almonds or coconut on top. I wanted to visit these people in their homes, hoping to create a more comfortable and intimate experience. I was surprised at how much I enjoyed seeing their homes and talking about construction, new furniture, red tape, city bylaws, et cetera. I hoped the homemade cakes would bring sincerity to the meetings and show some gratitude for their openhearted-ness. I enjoyed meeting these people so much. I loved seeing the tattoos; I didn't care so much about the quality of work. I wanted to hear their stories.

I was astonished at the lack of Christian symbolism used

in these tattoos. The cult of the saints is what makes the city of New Orleans so beautiful. Saints and religious symbolism are found all over the city — in architecture, city planning, even in the trees, where you can see shrines to saints such as St. Joseph (to protect the home) and St. Vitus (to protect from storms). Perhaps this is why people chose different and new symbols to express themselves. Maybe the wearers of these tattoos find the traditional motifs monotonous and want a new expression to represent a new city, a city of rebirth. There was a mix of emotions: anger, gratitude, confusion, pride, grief. Many affirmed the storm had changed them forever, and now, like in New York after 9/11, many no longer wanted to talk about Katrina. Three years later, as I met these people, offered pastry, and took pictures, the clean up was still in full swing, and people were moving on with their lives.

SPENCER was a lawyer (working with community organizations such as ACORN) for 22 years before he decided to pursue acting and painting. He lived in the Irish Channel and stayed in New Orleans during and after the storm alongside his cat and dog. He told me he "didn't have much to do" and

having tattooed himself in the past, he gave it another go.

This crude cat tattoo represents "Category 5," or "Cat 5," heard over and over again on the news about the approaching storm; it is meant to be tongue in cheek. When asked about the spirituality of his tattoos, he wrote that being a Buddhist, he had no "God" but that the tattoo made him feel at peace with what had happened and that it represented a visual expression of the fact that he'll never be the same.

ALMA MALECKAR has a tattoo of a flying po'boy that tattoo artist Josh White gave her in her living room after the storm. This tattoo represents how she feels about the city: "relaxed, fun and delicious … with a touch of irony." Spiritually the tattoo feels like a badge or shield. It makes her feel connected to the city and proud. She noted the religious undertones of the wings and calls the City of New Orleans "a sort of deity."

BRETT HOPKINS is a Jefferson Parish firefighter who worked during the aftermath of the storm. When asked about the meaning of his tattoo, Brett had none. His reply was that he thought it was "cool as crap" and that it bonded him to the other firefighters he worked with, as they had all gotten one. The phrase "I know what it means," is a common post-Katrina expression.

KARIN'S tattoo is very straightforward — NOLA. New Orleans, Louisiana. Upon visiting Karin at her mother's place, I could see the construction going on in their home. Her mother made a lovely meal and fed me while, in the other room, Karin filled out the questionnaire that I brought for each person who volunteered to be part of this project. Karin admits she is not the tattoo type; however, she decided to get the tattoo when it was time for her to move away from New Orleans for college.

"When I had to move after the hurricane, I was completely miserable! The 3 months I was away from here after the storm are lost months of my life, and the hurt of the whole city and community destroys me. My tat has helped me deal with that." Karin says that the connection she has to the city is a spiritual one: "I don't have any religious affiliations or beliefs, really, but I believe in enjoying your life to the fullest. That's what this city allows me to do; that's what the tattoo means."

I met **KATIE** and **CHRIS** at the Maple Leaf Bar on Oak Street in the afternoon. The Maple Leaf is very well known for its live music. Upon entering the place, I was greeted by a rather large Great Dane.

Katie's fleur-de-lis symbolizes the struggles the city went through during and after Katrina and the rebirth of the city. Katie's home suffered a lot of fallen tree damage while her neighbor's home was ruined. Her family business had nine feet of water; it was a struggle to restore it to its former self. The tattoo acted as a point in time for Katie. Once she got the tattoo she felt "prepared to clean up and get going."

Chris's tattoo is a symbol used in Mardi Gras Indian patchwork worn by the New Orleans Mardi Gras Indian chief, Big Chief Bo Dollis of the Wild Magnolias. Chris was married by the chief in 1999 during Mardi Gras. Although Chris acquired the tattoo before Katrina, it means more to him now than it did before. Spiritually the tattoo made him feel connected to the tribe and the culture of the city.

DINO and **DINA** both work at the Audubon Zoo and have matching Katrina tattoos. The storm brought them closer together and both agree that they would "do it all over again to end up being together." The storm was the beginning of their "great adventure." Dino had no spiritual feelings surrounding the storm, nor did Dina, but she did say, "I didn't have much sense of a God before, but I now feel even less like there's something bigger out there."

MICHAEL loves the city of New Orleans and its football team, the Saints. Michael likes the fleur-de-lis because it has been used as a substitute for the cross and says the "city is his higher power." When asked if the tattoo had any healing qualities he replied, "No … just wanted to get stamped."

❸ Michael's brother **AARON** got a Buddha tattoo after the storm. For him it symbolized his need for peace after the storm, and he wanted to mark a significant point in his life.

❹ **JESSICA** is an artist and dollmaker. Her home burnt down during the storm. Her tattoo is of a fleur-de-lis surrounded by fire and waves and held together by an angelic winged being. Jessica wanted her tattoo to forge solidarity with others. She says, "I believe that when you give body space to an energy, it helps the energy to manifest and grow in your life.

I think that's why all these people got a New Orleans tattoo after Katrina." The tattoo makes her feel "centered in the city and marked on the inside as well as on the outside." Spiritually, the tattoo symbolizes protection and solidarity. Getting the tattoo made her feel "as if I was actually doing something real spiritually to aid in the recovery of the city." Jessica felt stunned and frightened after the storm but holds out a lot of hope and concern for the art community.

DEVIN'S Mardi Gras mask and crawfish represent family: ❺ "My Mardi Gras tattoo reminds me of the nights sleeping on St. Charles Avenue the night before Mardi Gras, just to get a good spot [for the parade]. My whole family — including aunts, uncles and grandparents — would spend Lundi Gras sleeping in the backs of parked pick-up trucks. My tattoos are a symbol of me being from New Orleans. I want to show how proud I am of where I come from and nothing can keep me from coming back."

Spiritually, Devin remarked, "Honestly, I felt closer to God after the storm! I didn't pray much prior to Katrina. Now I pray much more and feel closer to God."

When I met **TOM TUFT**, I immediately recognized his tat- ❻ too. It is of the markings left on all the houses by the National Guard. Tom noticed that a lot of people were removing them from their homes, and he wanted to preserve the image. The red symbolizes blood and death, the 1422 is the number of deaths in New Orleans alone.

Tom was in Ohio working during the storm and watched it all take place on TV. He rushed back to New Orleans, and when he arrived, he noticed the loud silence. No birds, no locusts, no dogs barking.

After Katrina, Tom feels closer to God and often looks at

his tattoo in prayer. The tattoo has given Tom closure and the ability to move on.

DAVID ARTHUR was a member of the 82nd Airborne in his youth. The 82nd Airborne helped provide the citizens of New Orleans with protection. This tattoo gave David a sense of pride in the city but also in the airborne division he once belonged to. David made the decision to "stand and fight, not throw in the towel and give up." After the storm David felt further away from God: "Can't understand how that could be unleashed upon a city and its people."

❼ All of **LAURITA'S** tattoos honor her ancestors: "After the Hurricane, I read an autobiography of Assata Shakur. It is about the whole Panther struggle and representation of the people. It made me think of how the blacks were treated after Katrina, so I came up with this idea of a tattoo. The 'power to the people' fist coming out the swamp … the fleur-de-lis shining like the sun. Also, on my wrist is an Endinkra symbol called Kawake which means bravery, fearlessness and valor."

Katrina made Laurita feel much closer to her community and God and inspired her to "do more community organizing in New Orleans, to help change the racial issues here and everywhere … but starting at home."

When asked about the religious meaning of her Katrina tattoo, **KATHRYN** answered, "Religion is a form of social control … my 'God' is me." Her tattoo is a Greek phrase which translates to "the happiness brings the sadness."

"I wanted to regain the control I lost in my life due to Katrina. The pain of receiving the tattoo directly explains the meaning of the tattoo."

AVIVA didn't live in New Orleans before the storm. After Katrina hit, she was given an opportunity to volunteer with a relief group.

She writes, "My tattoo symbolizes my relationship, perspective and feelings about New Orleans as an entity. The snake is viewed as both a deceptive creature as well as a wise one. New Orleans is a wise old city with a rich history and a deep knowledge, but I have experienced so much deception here, both by individuals and by groups who are corrupt. The snake symbolizes a rebirth when it sheds its skin. I came to New Orleans after Katrina, during the difficult beginnings of its rebirth. In the story of Adam and Eve, the snake represents temptation and sin, sin manifesting itself in pleasure. New Orleans is a city based on worldly pleasure and is proud of who it is, despite others' judgments."

LINTON is a social worker for the city of New Orleans. He wrote of the symbolism of his tattoo, "The tattoo is the sign made on my house by the first responders. This was what I focused on when I tried to make sense of things after the storm. To me it means a hex sign, a modern day mark of Cain, symbolic of lambs' blood for an ironic Passover."

When asked how it made him feel, he replied, "I thought the mark would always be on me anyways, the physical hurt corresponds to the spiritual hurt. Also, I think it's sort of sexy."

When I asked **JASMINE** if her mosquito tattoo had any healing qualities, she replied, "*Very much!!!* That was the only reason I got it, to get it all out of my skin, heart, brain and soul. After Katrina there were many still pools of water and the mosquitoes bred instantly. That's what I connected to the storm."

SANDY'S tattoo represents the X's left on the houses by rescue personnel. She explained what the Egyptian scarab beetle meant for her: "The dung beetle pushes the dung across the desert floor, looking like the round sun, pushing it into a new day. Hope, life continues. Something old used to continue life."

When asked if she felt closer to God after Katrina, she replied, "I'm not a very religious person. There were times I prayed. There were times I felt abandoned here in this mess, but have not found God since the storm. I will say, it was biblical what went on here in terms of disaster. It was post-apocalyptic. You could see the Milky Way for the first time in the city. It was beautiful. It made me feel small and in tune with nature. Ironic, I suppose."

⑩ LIZ'S tattoo has no spiritual meaning for her, and after the storm she began to doubt the existence of God. The tattoo gives her a sense of pride in her Russian heritage and her love for the city she grew up in.

ALLIE'S feelings about God and the storm mimic Liz's. Her beautiful tattoo is of the famous New Orleans water meter. It gave her an enormous sense of "pride and empowerment."

PATTIE HALL'S son is a tattoo artist in San Francisco. Eight years ago, he gave her a tattoo of "New Orleans" written in script in the middle of a big red heart. At the time it made her feel "tuff," but since the storm it has taken on a new meaning of pride. She witnessed her neighbors in the French Quarter come together when the power was out and share medical supplies and food until rescuers arrived. She is grateful for the Katrina experience and remarked at how people stayed in the city for their pets. The National Guard wouldn't let people evacuate with their pets, but quickly changed their minds a few days later when they realized no one would leave otherwise. The tattoo provides no spiritual meaning for her, but Pattie is a proud Christian and always feels close to God.

THIS PROJECT REVEALED GOD AND the sense of the Holy by showing me the experience of Grace. My theology of Grace has changed as I have witnessed genuine experiences of both actual and sanctifying Grace. I have learned that Grace comes at times of destruction, chaos and death, and not just times of achievement, happiness and gratitude. I found that some people lost their faith in God when faced with Katrina while others found hope in community, strength, healing, closure, peace along with feelings of anger, loss and pain. The tattoos mean many things, but they revealed a Grace experience in all the people I spoke to. I discovered that believers and non-believers both felt a tremendous impact on their lives and a need to symbolize it in some way. Tattooing was the medium chosen for this expression, and God can be found in the creativity and imagination of these symbols.

This essay started out as a project about tattooing as healing but ended up being about both healing and the Grace experience. The experience of Grace is a human experience; it is real in our triumphs and failures and it belongs to us and to God.

SEPTEMBER 14, 1722

We are working hard here to repair the damage which the hurricane has caused …

SEPTEMBER 19

Today the two men accused of having plundered the storehouse were questioned and they confessed everything …

SEPTEMBER 20

A decree was issued this morning by which the commandants and the directors *order that all the inhabitants of this place must have their houses or land enclosed by palisades within two months or else they will be deprived of their property and it will revert to the company* …

SEPTEMBER 23

Counsel was held concerning the two men accused of having plundered the stores *and who had been questioned on the 19ᵗʰ of the present month. They were condemned to be hanged and to be strangled until life was extinct. This sentence was executed the same day, at four o'clock in the afternoon.*

From the Journal of DIRON D'ARTAGUIETTE (translated by Newton D. Mereness, 1916)

Ⓠ

"These troops are fresh back from Iraq, well
trained, experienced, battle tested and under my
orders to restore order in the streets … They have
M-16s and they are locked and loaded. I have one
message for these hoodlums: these troops know
how to shoot and kill and they are more than
willing to do so if necessary and I expect they will."

Governor Kathleen Blanco, September 1, 2005

Ⓡ

Standing outside the Walgreen's
with a stone in my hand
Standing outside with a stone in my hand
I ask myself will Jesus understand?

Chris Thomas King, from the song
"What Would Jesus Do?" (on the CD *Rise*),
recorded September 4, 2005

PART THREE
Loss.

S

We wonder if our northern friends form an adequate idea of a
rainy day in N. Orleans — and above all of an autumnal rainy
day. They imagine perhaps that our showers consist of the
contents of a single surcharged cloud, saturating the earth with
grateful moisture, and refreshing all nature with the effusion —
imparting a delightful coolness to the atmosphere, and filling
it with fragrance. How terribly they are mistaken. Our rains are
downright tropical torrents, following successively for two, three,
or four days, or it may be a week, converting our streets to rivers,
soaking and penetrating the innermost recesses of our dwellings,
covering every thing with humidity — veiling the bright sun
and enveloping the cheerful face of the Heavens in unrelieved
obscurity. Such a day we have before us. Miserably dull, heavy,
gloomy and insupportable. Not a moment's interval from its
pluvious violence, unless when the showers are for an instant
quenched by a rapid gleam of lightning, followed by a startling
peal jars that [sic] most unpleasantly upon our nervous system.
This is decidedly the most hypochondriac weather we have
witnessed for a long time, and we do not marvel at the suicidal
propensities of Englishmen, if, as 'tis said, they are doomed
annually to submit in their misty climate to the autumnal horrors
we now experience.

Saturday Morning
October 7, 1837
The New Orleans Bee

On Friday we experienced a severe gale accompanied by incessant
torrents of rain. The wind rose towards evening and blew with
a violence truly frightful. The effects of the tempest have been
severely and extensively felt. The whole of the back part of the

city was and still continues submerged. Four steamboats were thrown on shore, viz: the Merchant, Columbia, Mobile and Pontchartrain; the first is now lying immediately behind the house of Mr. Girodean, and the three others were cast upon the public road leading from the Railway to the Lake. These boats are totally destroyed. Almost all the dwelling houses at the lake have been either inceparably [sic] injured or entirely carried away by the violence of the gale. — Eight or ten alone remain standing — among them the Pontchartrain Hotel, the Arch.d. [?] Hotel and few others which have received such serious injury that considerable repairs will be required. The Rail road is inundated from Gentilly to the Lake. The building at the entrance of the Bayou was overturned and an individual (name unknown) was killed in its fall. In one of the ladies bathing houses the woman who kept the establishment saved herself with difficulty, but was compelled to become a spectator of the death of her child aged 12 years, without the power of rescuing him. A hut belonging to four fishermen was carried away. The inhabitants have not been heard of. — Happily the effects in town have not been so serious. The front and columns of the Citizen's Bank, in process of construction, were thrown down. It is said that the St. Charles Street Hotel was heard to crack … Various houses in town have sustained more or less damage. The New Cemetery is inundated, and fifteen bodies still remain without a possibility of performing the rites of interment. Such are the details we have been enabled to collect respecting this disastrous event.

Monday Morning
October 9, 1837
The New Orleans Bee

The sudden rise of the Lake, and the overflow of its waters occasioned by the hurricane of the 7th inst. have added strength to the conviction we had entertained of the immense advantages derived from the labors of the Draining Company; for even during the utmost elevation of the torrent, the contents of the Girod canal were kept no less than four feet lower than those of the Bayou St. John. It is with regret we have learned, that certain unforeseen obstacles had prevented the formation of Levees for the protection of the lands subject to the operation, from any spontaneous irruption of the waters of the Lake. Had these embankments been completed, the inhabitants of faubourg Trêmé would have been as free from inundation as those in the centre of the city …

The contemplated embankments, will now be speedily undertaken, and their effect will be so much the more certain, as we already know the utmost possible elevation of the waters of the lake, and can raise the levee to a greater height than was before intended. — We can thus guard against the possibility of future inundations …

Wednesday Morning
October 11, 1837
The New Orleans Bee

BTG632 1

Cutlery 2

Ironworks, Lakeview 3

After Katrina
SANDRA BURSHELL

Rape of Closet 4

Wall Pattern #2, Gentilly 5

Lampshade, Lakeview 6

Sofa, Lakeview 7

Put your nose up to the door, I told my daughter, and take a good sniff. This, I tell her, is what Katrina smelled like, what the whole city smelled like, in the days after. We were peering through the locked doors into the nave of St. Francis Cabrini Catholic Church, in the Vista Park section of Gentilly along Paris Avenue.

The interior of the church was a ruin of piled pews in the nave, as if prepared for a bonfire, in front of the dramatic sanctuary beneath its flying buttresses. I took a photograph through thick leaded glass I was tempted to break for a bet-

In the Brown Zone With Mother Cabrini

MARK FOLSE

ter view, given that the Archdiocese could clearly care less. I was only stopped by the thought of all the Humvees full of National Guard I had seen on Robert E. Lee. There was no sign of them here on Paris Avenue, no sign of life at all, but something stayed my hand.

My father led the design team for this church, helped apply the gold leaf to the ceiling with his own hands when funds ran low. I recall standing as a very small child in the back and watching him climb perhaps fifty feet of scaffolding to reach the top of the buttresses to inspect some work. To a very small child it seemed as if he had ascended the very ramparts of heaven to consult with God about the progress of the work on His house. It is one of the most vivid memories of my childhood, one I can call up clearly at any time.

My reverie was interrupted again by the smell as I pressed my eye to a window close to the crack in the door. Smell, I told my own child: smell this. Remember this smell, remember what happened to your new home, to the church your grandfather built; remember it as clearly as I remember your grandfather at the gates of heaven so you can tell your own children some day.

So much of the city is still in danger of being reduced to memory. Sidney J. Folse, Jr., A.I.A., was a prominent architect, a president of the New Orleans Chapter of the A.I.A. at the height of the battle of the Riverfront Expressway. He designed the Rivergate, and I marveled at the model of the Superdome that was central to his office at Curtis & Davis on Canal Street in the 1960s.

The Rivergate is gone, replaced by Harrah's. Beneath it somewhere is no doubt the tunnel dug for the riverfront expressway to cross Canal, the expressway my father helped to prevent. Given the life cycle of stadiums it is certain that within my lifetime the Superdome will be reduced to a memory. There will be so little left of my father in this city soon, only the memories of people who knew him, and with each passing year there are fewer to recall his name over a drink or a meal in the way Orleanians invoke our ancestors, with some fond anecdote at the table.

The only things that will remain in New Orleans from the hand of one of its prominent architects of the 20th Century will be a starkly modern house at 17 Egret Street in Lake Vista, just small enough in square footage to be at risk as a tear down in the land of McMansions, and this church.

Ten months after the flood Cabrini Church shows no sign

of any remediation. The smell is enough to know. The Archdiocese has apparently locked it and left it to rot, the pews piled up like bones in the oven of a raised tomb. Perhaps they plan to return in a year and sweep the remains into the drawer just as we clean out our family tombs, to make way for the new.

Or perhaps the bulldozers will come, if the neighborhood remains as it appears today, as still and silent and monochrome as a New Orleans cemetery on a hot August afternoon. Someone righted the toppled Virgin behind the church, and placed a small offering of artificial blooms in each of the urns that flanked the statue. Someone has come back, if only for an afternoon. But as I look over the open ground behind the church and school and the blocks of homes beyond, I don't see them. I don't see anyone.

Today, Mother Cabrini stands water stained near the impending ruin that bears her name, a fitting monument to the first American saint in a town thick with saints but abandoned by America, in a neighborhood where the homogeneous brown silence of the flood seems little changed since September, in a place where the water stood so high there are no rescue marks on the front of homes; instead, stroked zeros were marked on the roofs to show aircraft which homes were searched.

I read Vista Park homeowner Tim's Nameless Blog regularly. I know that people are coming back to the neighborhood that stands across Paris Avenue. Today I don't see them, even as a few blocks away Tim wrestles a push mower around Pratt Park and other neighbors work to bring the place they called home back from the disaster that stands in stark silence all around me.

If these places are saved, it will not be through the New Orleans Recreation Department saving Pratt Park or the Archdiocese of New Orleans saving Cabrini. It won't be the city or the U.S. Army Corps of Engineers or even the grace of God. New Orleans will be saved only because people who love these places, this city, insist on saving them. They will do it on their own, whatever it takes. They are the descendants of the immigrants Mother Cabrini ministered to here, people who were not afraid to go into the unknown, into the heat and the funk of this place called New Orleans and make it their home. Their great grandchildren will do it again.

Mother Cabrini, pray for them.

"In some ways the past is still present [in New Orleans] in ways if you grow up in New York, everything, your past is erased, physically erased. The school I went to, the houses I lived in, all of them, they are all gone. Here you can sort of see, it seems to me, the past over a lifetime. It's a very special quality and a very unusual one to see. It makes me feel sad … I think it's beautiful and tragic and moving and joyful."

Robert Stone,
March 13, 2008, at Tulane U.

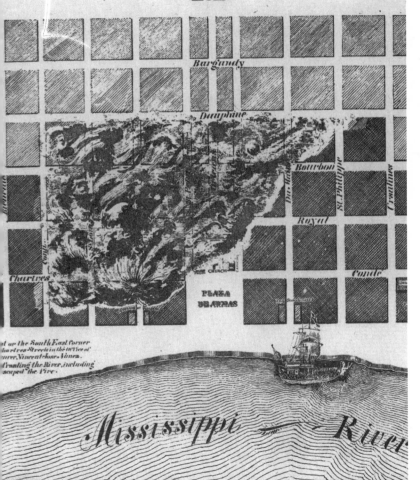

PLAN

showing the boundaries

OF THE

—— great Conflagration of New Orleans ——

on the 21st of March

1788.

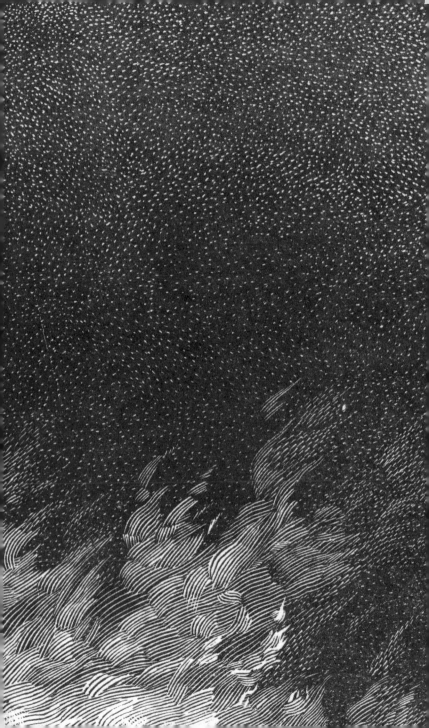

My memories of the place only go back as far as July of 1995, when I moved in cattycorner 3700 Magazine Street. Certainly the business long predated that hellish summer, but from 1995 to 2005, it was a corner grocery, package liquor store, and po'boy stand all rolled into one — all of it safely encased in the dilapidated two-story and formerly dirty white building that we all knew simply as Jennie's. Today, however, while that iconic building is still there, still looming awkwardly over Magazine Street, Jennie's is gone.

Jennie's Grocery: R.I.P.

JENNIFER A. KUCHTA

At some point over the years she became a dirty yellow building, and at some other point a dirtier yellow building when two men painted her that "newer" yellow by painting right over the years of dust and exhaust and grime and blood that clung to the old yellow. And in the span of those ten years, Jennie's changed hands a couple of times. Who knows who the original Jennie was or is, or where she went when she left the place, leaving only her name behind and swinging over the doorway, or if she ever even existed. The place was always Jennie's Grocery, always run by one set of Asians or another. There was always another Not Jennie smiling away behind its battered counter, peering through its scratched and smeared Plexiglas, always keeping one eye on the customer at hand

and one on whoever roamed the tiny space, prowled the narrow aisles. Until Katrina that is.

But before I get to that and before I wax all nostalgic on you, let's be honest for a second. Jennie's was not for the weak of heart, not for the Uptown ladies or well-heeled tourists. She was often one scary, sketchy place — just what we proletarian folk come to expect from a corner grocery in New Orleans. Before I quit smoking for the third (and final) time in July 2005, I spent plenty of time dodging Magazine Street traffic to buy my smokes. Jennie's was much smaller inside than one would expect. Her crammed little space held two or three rows of shelves, a couple of beverage coolers, and a worn out display-case counter with "bullet proof" glass around everything but the space near the register. While the pickings were slim and usually outdated, she offered cigarettes by the pack or individually, stale white bread, cheap cookies, chips, beer, and po'boys — all the typical corner store sundries.

Slipping through those open gates and through those flimsy, flapping wooden doors, one was sure to come face to face with some strung-out crack whore, some mean motherfucker bangers cursing at and pounding on the one standing video arcade (Galaga?), some dirty and often shoeless kids touching everything and buying nothing, and some variously employed and unemployed menfolk buying tallboys and 40s for breakfast, lunch and dinner.

Living diagonal to the place, I bore witness to all sorts of mayhem: blood left behind in the aftermath of stabbings, tons of fights — men, women, men and women, school kids, pit bulls — parents beating the piss out of their kids, women just screaming and screaming the way women do when they're drunk, scared, mad, insane, beaten. But the daily gatherings of drunks were what made Jennie's *Jennie's*. At all hours of the day and night despite the "no loitering" signs that graced the sides of the building, the sounds of drunken laughter and anger forever echoed across Magazine Street and into my house and ears.

In the ten years I knew Jennie's, Magazine Street grew up around her and got all gentrified. Away went the abandoned Laundromat that eventually went fine dining. Straight to hell went the rental house full of devil worshippers, and in first came skateboards, then fancy clothes for ladies, then some for metrosexuals, and now it's wedding gowns. The other corner grocery down the street eventually became a chichi linens shop. Along with those few changes came *way* upscale jewelry stores, art galleries, children's clothing stores, a plethora of boutiques, and a pilates studio. Even the Jetgo gas station got a makeover. But not Jennie's. She stayed weathered and worn and falling down bit by bit — the battered wife of Magazine Street.

Don't get me wrong, Jennie's was never so bad that you hoped she would just shut down and go away or burn to the ground. The chaos was pretty much confined to that one corner, a corner you could avoid if you wanted to, if you weren't having nicotine fits or delirium tremens. After all, she served as a backdrop for some rap video, and she graced the cover of the Dirty Dozen Brass Band's *Buck Jump*. Hell, she was how I directed people to my house: "You know where Jennie's is at? On Magazine?" But when Jennie's did finally go down, she went down fast — faster than a two-dollar whore.

ALMOST TEN YEARS TO THE day that I moved in diagonally from Jennie's, Chieu Ha Do was gunned down behind the counter of her own store at about one-thirty in the afternoon — on a Tuesday. A goddamn Tuesday. Shot in the back over who knows what real or imagined injustice. Some lousy, cowardly fucker waltzed into the place and killed that woman in cold blood as she ran for the back of the store, ran for her husband's help, and then that bastard waltzed right back out onto Magazine Street and somehow disappeared into the crowd, which was surely made up of mostly white and middle-class Uptown ladies and tourists.

Police cruisers lined up as far as the eye could see; yellow crime scene tape stretched around the four corners of the intersection. I saw the woman's husband on his knees and barefoot on the dirty, filthy sidewalk, hands clenched to his chest and sobbing. I saw them carry her body out; I saw the relatives come and scream and cry and grasp onto each other. Jennie's went down in the worst way possible.

After weeks of flowers and memorials tucked into the bars of her padlocked metal gates, Jennie's came back briefly for a day or two, but not really, and then came Katrina, the final nail in her proverbial, once-white coffin.

THAT TWO-STORY SHANTY TOWN weathered the hurricane better than I expected. In fact, she was the one thing in the area I was prepared to find leveled. She was sans some asbestos tiles and part of her balcony railing, but she was still there. And while I saw her roof get replaced and her railing come back and some other changes going on, a good two decade's worth of repairs being made, I didn't notice when exactly Jennie's just wasn't Jennie's anymore. That big white sign with the black and red lettering was just gone one day, and in its stead was Amelia Market.

Amelia Market — it just didn't roll off the tongue quite right. But it was, at least for a while, a restaurant of sorts, a sandwich shoppe perhaps — no po'boy stand, no Asians, no gangbangers. Certainly a place the Magazine Street frequenters of the anti-corner grocery sort would find a vast improvement. And I'll admit, at first, I did, too. At the very least the transformation meant (most likely) no shootings. It meant (hopefully) safety. The corner's silence meant more sleep. It meant (less importantly) further rising property values. But before I go all landed gentry on you, let me lay the truth of the matter down. The place was all fancy menu boards and nice new curtains. It was cooks in checkered pants, cute little deli tables et al., but the place was hardly ever open. And when it was open, there was no one there.

Perhaps the problem was simply post-Katrina New Orleans. Or perhaps it was that anyone back in this part of town knew about the murder. Or perhaps it was the white guy who sat outside on a stool all day long — trying to look threatening — daring anyone to cross that street and come on in. Or maybe it was the heavyset chef-looking guy who faithfully put out the signboard each morning but seemingly forgot to ever open the gates. Yes, those stripy curtains billowed in the breeze, but the gates stayed locked. Maybe it was a front for the Cajun Mafia; maybe it was a brothel. Maybe they were running numbers.

Pretty soon even the signboard didn't go out. Stool Man disappeared. Neon signs burned away in the interior, behind the windows, but the place was plain old closed.

AFTER MONTHS OF SILENCE, NO drunks, no gunshots, I started waking to the sounds of reggaeton and the excited banter of Mexican workers. Power sanders buzzed away at all hours of the day, tossing decades of leaded paint into the air. One day I came home and that building towered over Magazine Street in the gayest shade of purple ever. But no Jennie's, no Amelia Market, no nothing. Curious folks pressed their noses to the windows, but the building just sat silent and empty, rising like Liberace's tombstone out my front window.

Soon the biggest FOR RENT sign possible went up. Seven-hundred and some odd feet were ready to rent. And she sat and sat. And the longer she sat, the more I hoped that anyone even remotely thinking about renting the place (of living out their life-long dream of having their own little place to sell their own little wares, be their own boss and all that shit), was planning on the glory of selling single Sundance smokes and malt liquor, of squeezing the staling loaves of bread, and pondering the many varieties of po'boys they could concoct in their very own corner grocery, package liquor store, and po'boy stand all rolled into one.

After all, every structure up and down Magazine had changed and for the most part survived, survived the years and survived the hurricanes. It all changed, it went upscale, or at least up the scale. But that corner sans Jennie's went NO PLACE. I became convinced that *only* another Jennie's would find success — would bring the corner back to life. But I was wrong. And I sure as hell never expected the bongos.

TAPAS. YES. TAPAS. WHAT WAS once Jennie's Grocery is now a tapas bar and Latin bistro. Has been for some time now. When people ask what happened to "that store where that lady got murdered," I tell them, "It's a tapas bar." And they say, "Topless bar? That's odd." And I say, "No, tapas. T-A-P-A-S." Topless bar ... I wish.

Today, little square tables crowd the sidewalk while ceiling fans whirl overhead, trying to stir up the oppressive July air. Before the summer heat came on, the place was always crowded. Sometimes folks lined up around the corner waiting for one of the few tables, but I've never been there. In fact,

I've probably stood on that corner only three times in the four years since Katrina. Why? I don't know. Maybe I feel like the restaurant is cheating, like it's disrespectful somehow to what was once there — to a woman murdered trying to turn a buck and to a long-standing New Orleans corner grocery. Maybe in time it would have been Jennie's again. Or Emily's or Megan's or even Ivan's. Maybe.

For the most part, it is a great improvement, but it's not the same. Sure, there are the peals of laughter that grow in intensity as closing time nears and the late night stacking of chairs and tables. While the rest of Magazine Street sleeps, slamming car doors and slurry goodbyes sound beneath my living room window. And let's not forget those bongos. Bongos. For those not in the know, with bongos come chanting and yelling and laughter that rises and rises — all of it increasing in pitch and fury and frenzy until suddenly, just when I can't take it anymore, BAM! Eleven o'clock comes like a knife ripping through the night, cutting off all sound. Dead silence.

And in that silence, if I listen hard enough, I can almost hear the sounds of breaking glass and flesh. Oh, and genuine drunken laughter, belly deep and fueled by nothing but the promise of the next drink. Laughter that belongs to men and women who want nothing more than a cool drink on a sweltering July night. Listen. Man, it's been a long, silent time.

U

There used to be a pelican in the neighborhood of
Jackson Square.

We used to attach considerable interest to that bird
… But the bird simply went the way of all flesh;
for an aged man who haunts the Passage de Saint-
Antoine declares that he sees its ghost sometimes of
clear nights, perched on the head of Gen. Jackson. He
knows it is a ghost, because the stars shine through it.

And the bird says — according to the ancient —
something to the following effect, shortly before the
midnight hour —

"I was a symbol. I am still a Symbol in my ghostliness.
I betoken the old-fashioned life of the Pelican State
that is passing away. I represent the quaintness that
is dying out, and the antiquated thing that shall soon
become as ghostly as myself. The old city is becoming
Americanized; and I am glad that I am dead."

from LAFCADIO HEARN,
"The Pelican's Ghost" (1880)

There were hardly any children in my old neighborhood, the Faubourg Marigny. By 1999, when I first moved into a single-shotgun house next to the train tracks on Press Street, the neighborhood was already in the throes of some serious gentrification. Homes were owned by a tight circle of career landlords and a large population of gay men. The renters, like me, were young and worked in the service industry or in the arts. Babies were had mostly on accident. I remember only

We Live on Both Sides

SARAH DEBACHER

three neighborhood children. They lived blocks apart. Their parents were either contemplating a move to another neighborhood closer to the uptown parochial schools, or they were home-schooling them in coffee shops. I can't say I paid much attention to the absence of children when I was renting in the Marigny, but when my husband and I first moved away from the high-cost homes near the French Quarter to our post-Katrina renovated double in Holy Cross on the other side of the Industrial Canal, I remember thinking, "Oh, yeah: kids!" And then: "Oh: kids." And finally: "Oh: *boys*."

Damone was the first boy I met in our new neighborhood. He lived with his mom, an uncle, and an older brother who was under house arrest and who was nonetheless making a good living selling weed out of their side of the shotgun-double they rented across the street from us. At the time, there was only one other boy besides Damone living within a three-block radius: Don. Don's father was fanatically religious and didn't let him do anything Damone considered fun, so Damone spent his afternoons smacking the sidewalk with Mississippi driftwood, rolling an orphaned wheel he'd found in some ditch or jumping the fence by the abandoned Holy Cross School and pretending things that required a lot of cussing. From the kitchen window where I watched, I could tell that Damone was both supremely bored and supremely lonely. So one day, my husband and I offered to give him some work.

The day that Damone was meant to come over to cut the grass, he and Don both showed up. From the sofa where I was grading essays for my summer-school job, I could hear Damone and Don deal-making outside the door. Don had brought the mower, so *clearly* he deserved to get paid. But it was *Damone* who'd gotten the job, he pointed out, so even if Don *did* do most of the work, it was still only fair that they split things, fifty-fifty.

I should say that I liked Don. He was a smart kid and a vegetarian of his own accord. He liked to ask my husband about what it was like to live in England. Damone, I didn't care for so much. He threw tantrums. He threw his Crocs in the street and told his little cousin to go pick them up. One day, when he was hanging out with some of his other cousins, he threw an empty can of Chek strawberry drink in the drainage ditch by my house. When I came out the front door, I was fuming, and yet I was conscious of who I was to them: this crazy white lady who'd moved in with her tall, funny-talking husband. This outsider. This bitch.

"Would you please pick up the soda can you just threw in my yard?"

Damone looked at his friends, at the can, then back to his friends. "That's not mine."

"I didn't ask if it was yours," I said. "I asked if you would please pick it up."

Damone smacked his teeth. "I didn't throw it down so I'm not picking it up."

After a moment of jockeying, each boy standing around daring each other to do something I'd asked them to do, one of Damone's older cousins smacked his teeth, picked up the can, said, "Sorry, Miss," and looked at me in a way that said, "It *is* Damone's can, but you know how Damone be trippin' sometimes." I knew.

The day of the lawn-mowing, when Damone and Don rang the doorbell, I steeled myself for some of Damone's worst behavior, but I was hopeful that the promise of fifteen dollars for an hour's work would keep him respectful, keep him in line. I opened the door, told the boys I'd be inside if they needed anything, and got back to work, listening for wrong-doing, waiting for something to go wrong.

The mower wouldn't start. Don was quiet as he pushed the primer-button again and again, as he pulled and re-pulled the starter-chain. Damone smacked his teeth, asked him did he really know how to work that thing, and said, "Man, it's too hot. Let's ask for something to drink."

When I went to the door, I did so with a look on my face that I hoped showed my disappointment. "I hear you want something to drink," I said, looking out the door, past them, at the unmowed grass. "Doesn't look like you've gotten much done." Don explained the trouble with the mower, said it might just need a minute to rest, was all. Damone said they just needed something cool to drink, then they could get down to work. "We're gonna do a good job," he said. "You'll see."

I let the boys in the side door and told them to take off their shoes if they wanted to go past the runner-rug in the entry. I hoped they wouldn't want to. Don said, "We'll stay here."

Damone kicked off his Crocs. "I wanna see your house," he said.

I felt self-conscious immediately. I knew from walking past his house that Don slept on a bunk bed in the front room of one half of a three-room shotgun double; he'd been lying on the bottom bunk with a book, the front and back doors open so he could catch a breeze. There was no air-conditioning in Don's home. Damone lived with five and sometimes six people in four rooms—their half of a rented shotgun double. My husband and I had converted our shotgun double into a single residence with two bedrooms, two bathrooms, two living rooms, and a kitchen with Energystar appliances. It wasn't so much that I didn't want Damone to see our open floor-plan, our many nice things; I didn't feel bad about what we had (at least this is what I tell myself). It was just that I knew Damone would get the wrong idea. He would think we were rich.

"You can see the kitchen if you want," I said, walking ahead, opening our IKEA cabinets. I took out two plastic Mardi Gras cups. "You want ice?" I asked.

"If y'all got it."

I opened the freezer drawer on the bottom of our new refrigerator and filled the cups with cubes from the ice-maker. I pulled the Brita pitcher from the fridge and poured two cups. Damone looked around. He seemed to be most interested in what was around the corner from the kitchen, in the front rooms, which paralleled the street. Those were the rooms he saw from his front porch. I imagined him imagining our lives as he looked at our house from across the street, just as I had imagined his when the parole officer came by to check on his older brother, when his mother got in a screaming fight with an ex and threw his clothes on the street, when things were quiet and I'd see Damone rapping to himself and looking across the street at our house. What did he imagine of me, of us?

"Can I see the front?" he asked, already moving from the kitchen to the dining room.

"Sure," I said, still holding the two waters. "But then you got to get back to work because I have a lot of work to get done, myself."

I watched him take it in: our open floor plan, our pocket doors, the new and matching furniture. "This is nice," he said. "I like your table."

Don called from the back room to say he was going back outside. Damone was smacking his teeth again, quietly this time. He was standing in the dining room now, looking through the space where a wall used to be, into the study. "Man," he said. "Who lives in that room?"

"That's the study."

"Like a library?"

"Sure, like a library."

"Where do the other people stay?"

"What other people?"

"You know — the other people?"

"There are no other people. It's just my husband and me."

Damone seemed perplexed, like he was struggling to make sense of it. In his house, there was a wall between one side and the other; in his house, bedrooms opened onto bedrooms — his cousin's onto his onto his mom's; in his house, an open floor plan meant the absence of privacy, of lockable doors. Suddenly he turned and looked right at me. "Y'all live on both sides?" he said.

I handed him the two cups of water. "What do you mean?"

"I mean you live on *both sides*," he said.

I understood then: Damone was astonished that we lived in the whole house, just the two of us — just two people, eight rooms. It wasn't the first time I felt self-conscious about our relative privilege here in our new Lower Ninth Ward home, but it was the first time I saw how it was felt by this kid, this boy who lived on my street.

"Yes," I said. "We live on both sides."

Damone looked at me, smacked his teeth one last time, said, "Dang," took the cups from me, and went back out to mow our lawn.

I knew how he felt. I'd been looking forward to the presence of children in my neighborhood, in my life, and now that they were here — these boys with their nigga-this and fuck-that, with their sticks and littering and boy-things, with legacies of poverty, their overcrowded homes, with their always moving and their one pair of shoes — now that I was looking these boys in the eyes, really seeing how the legacies of their childhoods had turned them quiet, turned them loud, turned them vegetarian, turned them angry, *seeing* how these legacies were turning these boys into young men with a sense not just that life was unfair, but that it was unjust — now there was a part of me that wished I hadn't moved here, that wished I could just close the door, close the curtains, and look away.

Twenty years of artwork, some collected and much created by me on the easel that was a birthday present. Most of our treasured book collection, including the rare copies of Zola that we searched for and bought piecemeal over years, antique Peter Rabbit books I'd been saving to give my grandson all gone in a toxic soup. Boxes and boxes of books. All the family photos from my 50-plus years and the photos of ancestors who lived before my birth — all in storage. Three steamer trunks full of personal treasures. All the Christmas decorations, including a little cookie bell that our daughter made in kindergarten. The can full of ornaments that she picked out, one for every year of her childhood. A lot of her things were in there too. Her childhood treasures, her yearbooks, her graduation pictures. None of this compares to loss of life or loss of a family home. Doesn't come close. But still there is grief, enormous grief over the loss of those memories.

Breach of Contract

SAM JASPER

I can replace books. I can't replace photographs, paintings or ornaments. The greatest loss, however, was an intangible.

Two months after the storm, I attended a panel discussion on the mental health issues that were expected to show themselves in the aftermath. An elderly psychiatrist listened to the other panelists, then quietly said, "Yes, it's the loss of life and property that we grieve. We grieve the possible loss of our culture, our favorite places, our way of life. Nothing will ever be the same. However, what we will grieve most is the loss of our belief in a social contract between our government and our populace. It's a breach of trust. No one's talking about that, but after years of belief in something as fundamental to our civic sense of ourselves, a sense that we were part of something greater than just our little block or neighborhood, to suddenly find that we were naïve in our expectations— that is a shock and a trauma. It will be years before that grief abates, if ever."

So far it hasn't.

Katrina took away my laissez-faire attitude toward the abuses of our environment. She got in my face and *immersed* me in Mother Nature's drama. She taught me that humankind is a powerful force, whose actions reach much further than we seem to realize.

In My Face

TRACEY TANGERINE

Yes, Katrina was a tough, prophetic teacher. She caused enormous devastation, but she also provided a look into our near future … a future full of even greater destruction if humankind continues to turn a blind eye to the inevitable consequences of our reckless behavior.

Katrina urged me to rush to a screening of *An Inconvenient Truth*, where I learned about the extreme weather patterns associated with global warming, the cracking of the Earth here and flooding there. She encouraged me to read *Holding Back the Sea*, where I learned that oil dredging has been chewing up the Louisiana coastline. She caused me to think daily about the hazardous burning of fossil fuels, the warming of our atmosphere, the endangered species, the melting ice caps, the rising ocean levels.

Hurricane Katrina banished my comfortable ignorance, but she also gave me a purpose. She led me by the hand and said, "Speak out. Spread my message …"

As a doctor and healthcare provider, I began to note a dramatic increase in the number of death notices in the newspaper since Hurricane Katrina. This observation was supported further by the deaths of two staff people in my own department within a short time and anecdotal accounts of families going to more funerals than ever. Due to the lack of current state data concerning this problem, the City's Health Department engaged in a study to count the death notices posted in the *Times-Picayune* newspaper and compared it to a parallel period before Hurricane Katrina.

In order to validate our methodology, we compared the number of death notices printed in the newspaper in 2002 and 2003 to the published state data from death certificates. In both cases, the difference between the two was not statistically significant. In 2003, we averaged 924 deaths per month according to death notices. In contrast, for the first six months in 2006, New Orleans averaged 1,317 death notices per month. This means that approximately 7,902 citizens expired in the first six months of 2006, as compared to approximately 5,544 in the first six months in 2003. These observations ... strongly suggest that our citizens are becoming sick and dying at a more accelerated rate than prior to Hurricane Katrina.

We believe these findings are significant, but the City has reached the limits of its ability to research this important issue. It is critical that state and federal agencies immediately study these trends as well as the causes of death. This information can then be used to develop appropriate interventions.

We would also recommend that the federal government

establish an electronic National Death Registry system to track mortality rates after any disaster that involves massive evacuation and mobilization of people across state lines. In the case of Hurricane Katrina, New Orleans residents were required to evacuate to more than 40 states.

Dr. Kevin U. Stephens, Sr., Director of the City of New Orleans Health Department, March 13, 2007, testimony given to the U.S. House of Representatives

And yet, if it were granted a native in exile to return to the city
upon but one day of the year, that day would be All Saints,
le jour des morts, the home festival of the city, for it comes at
a season when there are few, if any, strangers visiting the place.
The denizens from other regions, without the sentiment of the
day in their hearts, make it a holiday for out-of-town excursions;
hunting parties, country jaunts. They have not their dead with
them … To people of the city, the real people of the city, as they
like to be called, not to observe the day means to have no dead, no
ancestors …

On the last day of October, the flower venders come, filling the
banquettes all around the churches and markets, securing stations
at the corners of the streets, where, under the flare of torches, they
sell their white chrysanthemum crosses, crowns, baskets later into
the night. There are never flowers enough, despite season, nature,
or artifice; how can there be when everybody, even to the beggars,
must have some; for even the beggars have their dead somebody
to remember, their grave somewhere to decorate. By daylight of
All Saints, the early church-goers say in quaint figure of speech,
that the city smells like a cemetery, meaning the fragrance of it
from the flowers everywhere …

To speak of it at all is to speak of it too much. The external, the
obvious features of it, are but as the undertaker's paraphernalia
to the sentiment of death. The aged ones, themselves so close to
death, white-haired, bent-backed, clasping their memorials in
palsied hands; the little ones tripping gaily along with carefully
shielded bouquet; the inmate from the almshouse hobbling
among the pauper graves; the wrinkled negro mammies and uncles
with their tokens; the coloured people going to their cemeteries;

the Italians, Spaniards, Portuguese, around their gaudily draped mausoleums; — one can only enumerate details like that …

The festival of the dead might be called the festival of the history of the city. Year after year from under their decorations of evergreens and immortelles, roses and chrysanthemums, the tombstones recall to the All-Saints pilgrims the names and dates of the past; identifying the events with the sure precision of geological strata. On them are chronicled the names of the French and Canadian first settlers; the Spanish names and Spanish epitaphs of that domination; the names of the émigrés from the French revolution; from the different West Indian islands; the names of the refugees from Napoleon's army; the first sprinkling of American names; and those interesting English names that tell how the wounded prisoners of Pakenham's army preferred remaining in the land of their captivity, to returning home. The St. Louis cemetery for the coloured people unfolds the chapter of the coloured immigration, and by epitaph and name furnishes the links of their history.

The first Protestant cemetery (very far out of the city in its day, now in the centre) bears the name of the French Protestant mayor and philanthropist, Nicolas Girod. It belongs to the Faubourg Ste. Marie period, and in it are found the names of the pioneers of her enterprise; of the first great American fortune makers, the first great political leaders, the brilliant doctors of law, medicine, and divinity, who never have died from the memory of the place. In it is to be found the tomb of that beautiful woman and charming actress, Miss Placide, with the poetical epitaph written for her by Caldwell; the lines which every woman in society in New Orleans, fifty years ago, was expected to know and repeat. The Mexican war is commemorated in it by a monument to one of the heroes and victims, General Bliss. The great epidemics make their entries year after year; pathetic reading it is; all young, strong, and brave, according to their epitaphs, and belonging to the best families. The epidemics of '52 and '53 date the opening of new cemeteries, in which the lines of the ghastly trenches are still to be traced.

The Metairie cemetery (transformed from the old race track) contains the archives of the new era — after the civil war and the reconstruction. In it are Confederate monuments, and the tombs of a grandeur surprising all previous local standards. As the saying is, it is a good sign of prosperity when the dead seem to be getting richer.

The old St. Louis cemetery is closed now. It opens its gates only at the knock of an heir, so to speak; gives harbourage only to those who can claim a resting-place by the side of an ancestor. Between All Saints and All Saints, its admittances are not a few, and the registry volumes are still being added to; the list of names, in the first crumbling old tome, is still being repeated, over and over again; some of them so old and so forgotten in the present that death has no oblivion to add to them. Indeed, we may say they live only in the death register.

GRACE KING,
New Orleans: The Place and the People,
1895

Helen was an artist, and her medium was film. She was best known for doing animation, but she also turned the camera on her own life. Her house flooded after Katrina, swamping a lot of reels. Back in August she helped organize a home movie screening and she showed one of her own family, salvaged from the flood. A lot of people would have thrown it away. Helen found beauty in the way the toxic waters had contorted it. New textures and shapes danced over images of her baby boy Francis, giggling and squirming. In her hands this ruined thing was transformed into an artifact even more valuable than before.

New Orleans Loss

EVE TROEH

Right after Katrina hit, Helen moved with Francis and her husband Paul to South Carolina. They stayed there about a year, struggling with the decision whether to return. Friends told me there was a postcard campaign, initiated by Helen, to convince them to return.

Both worried that pollution from the flood might make their young son sick. Paul is a family doctor, who served some of the poorest people in New Orleans. He worried about the environmental hazards, but just as much about the crime in the city after the storm.

They did come back, over the summer, and it felt like a

victory for the city. Their talent and energy were especially welcome. They moved into my neighborhood, just a few blocks away. Paul started working at a health clinic down the street. I'd see the three of them out for walks, Paul or Helen pulling Francis behind in a red wagon.

Two days ago someone broke into their house in the early morning hours.

Helen was shot and killed.

The police came to Paul at the house, blood leaking from several gunshot wounds, Francis in his arms.

It looks like Paul is going to live, and Francis is ok.

Helen's gone.

All of us who've come back to New Orleans know there's risk involved, on every level. The levees aren't rebuilt. The public systems are still broken. But for many of us, it's exciting that our collective human potential could change something destroyed into something beautiful.

Helen's death has turned that light bulb off for a lot of people. People like me, with professions and skills and enthusiasm we could take anywhere.

Now it doesn't seem clear that we're going to get a good return on our reinvestment here. I'm consumed with constant cost benefit analysis, with the costs racking up faster and faster as the death tally in the city grows, not just Helen, but every life lost.

I went by Helen and Paul's house. There's a shiny bicycle still locked to the railing of the front porch. People have left flowers all over the steps. A magic marker drawing of rainbows and hearts is tacked to the door.

It says: Let her rest. In peace.

But we're not sure when peace is going to come. Or how.

"We choose New Orleans."

AMANDA BOYDEN,
Babylon Rolling
2008

Ⓨ

"We must leave. Now."

IGNATIUS REILLY, in the conclusion of
John Kennedy Toole's *Confederacy of Dunces,*
written early 1960s, published 1980

"Stormy weather may come and go,
Mother Nature may put on her show,
Still in my mind there's nowhere else to go.
So baby won't you please come home?

New Orleans is where I want to stay,
Where I can play my music every night and day.

There's just nothing more than New Orleans."

"I Hope You're Comin' Back to New Orleans," written by
Joe Braun, performed by The New Orleans Jazz Vipers
on *Hope You're Comin' Back,* March 2006

PART FOUR
Home II.

"Our precious hearts are all shattered
Scattered across the land.
But I know that I am going back
To the place where I know who I am."

— Susan Cowsill, "Crescent City Snow"

Carry Me Home

MARK FOLSE

Last night I met the man who brought me home.

No, he didn't carry me on his back like St. Christopher or ferry me home in a boat or even loan me twenty bills. Still, it is because of him that I find myself here on the shores of my own personal Ithaca. The meeting that resulted was not as profound as it sounds. A sideman in the band I was listening to was introduced to the crowd, and in the moment, I knew who he was. Later, we spoke briefly like two men who discover they have a common friend or interest, as any two men in New Orleans, given time enough to talk, may likely find. And in that brief encounter, I closed the circle on a journey of twenty-one years.

My wife and a very old friend and I went to hear Ingrid Lucia sing at the d.b.a bar on Frenchman Street in the Faubourg Marigny just behind the French Quarter. For out-of-towners, this is where the locals hang, where the French Quarter of Tennessee Williams and William Burroughs still lives on just across Esplanade Avenue from the Vieux Carré. For the first set, we sat in a small window seat carrel and listened, having an animated conversation about this and that, a big trip to Europe we were planning. Every now and then, we'd fall silent and listen to Ingrid sing, or the quartet backing her wail. During the second set, we decided to move out into the main room and just listen to the music. My friend Eric and my wife grabbed some seats along the wall, and I settled in on the floor at their feet.

As we watched the group, I kept looking at the horn player. There was something so damned familiar about him, but I couldn't place it. This happens to me all the time since I returned to New Orleans. The city is full of people I knew in passing over twenty years ago, and I keep seeing faces I feel I might have known in the long ago. There was something about the trumpet player that told me: you know him from *somewhere*. Then the singer introduced him. And now, she said, we're going to feature Mark Braud on vocals.

It was then I knew. The name triggered a flood of memory. I was transported briefly from the floor of a small, dark nightclub in the Marigny to an auditorium at the North Dakota State University in Fargo, to late September of 2005 and the first days after the Federal Flood. My wife and I were alone in front. Most of the crowd sat to the back of the room, tentative and polite as any group of North Dakotans will mostly be. Like characters from a monologue by Garrison Keillor, they huddled like a herd against the back and side walls: none was going to push up too close to the bright lights in front and call attention to themselves.

My wife is from North Dakota, and we raised our children there. I had lived in that area for over a decade and away from

New Orleans for almost twenty years, but remained deep down a Crescent City boy. Clad in a Mardi Gras-colored rugby shirt and clutching a large purple, green and gold golf umbrella, I had brashly marched down to the front and plopped myself dead center, just one row back from the empty front. In the cold and dark of the North that dreadful September of 2005, I went to this concert like a lost soul stumbling into a church, desperate for some redemption. If there were to be any splash of holy water or waft of incense from the altar, I was going to be close enough to catch it.

My neighbors in Fargo were so sympathetic in those days in the warm way of Midwesterners, looking for me to explain what they saw but could not comprehend, to tell them why people would stay in such a place with or without a storm. For people only a few generations removed from the old country who have stayed for a century through the most miserable winters out of their love of where they live, you would think they would be as conscious of the power of place as any imaginary denizen of Yoknapatawpha County would, but they were not.

That love of place had nearly undone me in those days. I had spent the prior weeks like a man adrift, had been struggling not to drown in tears or burst into flame with anger. I was desperate to escape the television and Internet news, was anxious to hear the sound of a voice with a certain, familiar timber and turn of phrase. As kind as my Fargo friends had been, I longed to be in the company of people who had moved from rice gruel to gumbo before they could properly say the word, to feel the insistent rhythms of the second line, to witness fingers doing that peculiar boogie-woogie dance that is New Orleans piano, to hear a horn by turns plaintive and brash trumpet the familiar songs. At a time when it was not clear that home would ever be there to go to again, I wanted to be carried home.

The affair was a Red Cross benefit for the victims of Katrina. Someone in the Red Cross had managed to put the Troy Davis Quartet on the road doing benefits, raising money for the cause and giving these displaced musicians a role to play, doing what they know best — the music of New Orleans. Somewhere I have a clipping from the Fargo Forum newspaper reviewing the show. Sometime I will pull it out and read it again, but not today. There was only one moment in the show that will remain with me until the day I die and they carry me the few blocks down Canal Street to Greenwood Cemetery.

At a point late in the show, Mark Braud spoke briefly, looking not at the crowd but at the horn in his hand, of how the Red Cross had arranged for him to get in and out of the city and recover his instrument. Tonight was the first time he would play it since the flood. He said some more words about the city and its predicament, spoke of the losses of so many, but I was lost after he spoke of recovering his trumpet, transported into sorrow, all of the pathetic scenes from TV and the Internet rushed back at me like sudden flood waters. When I focused again, he had called the song and the band began to play "Do You Know What It Means to Miss New Orleans?"

They played it just a bit slower than the usual tempo, the drummer on brushes playing the soft and respectful cadence of a jazz funeral marching out. Between singing the verses and playing his horn Braud looked not at his audience but down at the stage, rubbing away what I knew were tears in his eyes, the same that clouded my own view of the stage. When he lifted his horn to his lips he played that song with the same sad joy musicians of his father's and perhaps his grandfather's generation had played it. Unlike most of the polite audience, I heard not one but the voice of a hundred trumpeters from New Orleans who were, that night in September 2005, somewhere other than home; I heard them like a chorus of the sanctified in heavenly white robes blowing draped horns to call all the children home; I heard in it the wobbly wail of a late night busker somewhere in the Quarter playing the Lincoln Center in his head.

I quietly wept. I don't know about the audience. I couldn't turn my head to look, as I might have with the training of a journalist to sweep the situation and look for the bit of color to add to the story, the picture in words of the crowd that might make the scene. That night I was that bit of color, one of the five men in that room for whom that song on that night in the fall of 2005 was not just a song but was like the wailing of the apostles after the Crucifixion and the later descent of tongues of fire onto their heads. And I was not the only one who was moved.

Next to me my wife listened and watched as Braud wiped at his eyes between singing and blowing. This Pentecost of the lost reached down and touched her as well. She told me later that in that moment she understood my earlier announcement that I wanted to, no, needed to go home to New Orleans, to a city at that time more than still half underwater and in near complete ruin. She understood that my past light-hearted remarks about emigrating to America from New Orleans were not a joke but a way of saying how much I needed to be home, that home was more than just where she and I and the kids lived but a very specific and irreplaceable point on the map. She had watched me the preceding weeks glued to the television and computer, sleeping maybe five hours a night and slowly unraveling in grief, and that night in Fargo saw that grief paraded on stage.

She told me it was then she knew that she had to let me come home.

And that was how I came to find myself sitting on the floor

of d.b.a watching Mark Braud playing his horn, just as I had sat in that Fargo auditorium two-and-a-half years earlier, and recognized him as the man who had brought me home. It wasn't as powerful a moment as the one in 2005, but I knew as I sat there and listened that I had closed a circle, completed the journey that began when I left the city New Year's Eve morning 1986. Seeing Braud there on stage closed the chapter that began with a weather forecast one Friday late in August two years ago and which I thought had ended when I crossed the Causeway on Memorial Day 2006 with the city skyline rising up from the horizon, but which did not really resolve itself until I shook Braud's hand, told him the story and thanked him for helping to bring me home.

It was a quietly anti-climatic moment. What does one say when a complete stranger comes up to you and says something like, "I just wanted to tell you you're the reason I'm home." He just looked at me with no particular expression on his face, then began to smile a bit as I told him the story in brief — living in Fargo, the concert and his story of recovering his horn and his tears as he sang the song, and how that had moved my wife to decide that yes, somehow, we would move to New Orleans. He was silent for a bit, trying to place my odd story in among the expected things people will say to a performer just off stage. He just kept nodding his head slightly as if I were still talking, until his face lit up with a broad smile and he said, "Well, welcome home man!" My own story all told, I couldn't think of another word myself. "You, too," I offered.

With that, I took my drink out into the street for a cigarette, and watched the crowd passing along Frenchman Street. I thought about the long journey to this evening, twenty one years almost to the day, to this night in a club listening to fantastic New Orleans music with an old, old friend and my wife the newest Orleanian. As Braud returned to the stage and I heard his horn from inside dueling with the coronet player up the block in the street band, and the music pouring out of the Spotted Cat where later I would catch the Jazz Vipers; while I watched the parade of tourists and the local regulars — the "Quarter rats" — and people dressed up for a just-once-in-a-while night on the town passing up and down the street and in and out of clubs; as I contemplated a plate of red beans and some fried okra at the Praline Connection to soak up the beer; as I stood there and the music and the scene and the thought of good food contended for my attention, the words from Cowsill's alt-country/folk anthem came to mind: "But I know that I am going back/to the place where I know who I am." I crushed out my cigarette and stepped back into the crowded club and the music to find my wife and friend, the last pieces I needed to put together the puzzle that is home, stepped into the heart of Frenchman Street Friday night, into the heart of New Orleans: home for certain and home to stay.

"I hope to die in my sleep, when the time comes, and I hope it will be in the beautiful big brass bed in my New Orleans apartment …"

from TENNESSEE WILLIAMS,
Memoirs (1972)

1

Last summer I was the poster girl for New Orleans. My picture ran in the Sunday paper with the headline "Generation K." I smiled, flanked by hot pink oleander and golden hibiscus.

In the interview I praised the city for its social warmth and tropical elegance. I declared it my goal to tell stories about its stumbling, slow recovery. I'd quit busing tables at an Uptown bistro so I could report full time.

Dear New Orleans: I'm Leaving You

EVE TROEH

My voice has been on NPR and other national outlets reporting on crime, housing, insurance, and tourism. But unlike most reporters who fly in for a few weeks at a time, I've lived here throughout. So when I go to the drug store, and chat with the drug store clerk, I'm not buying travel shampoo for my next assignment. She recognizes me. Last year on Labor Day she was crying. In the past, she'd have thrown a big family picnic, but her house had flooded to the roof. Some of her family died. The rest left.

No more family, no more picnics.

Then there's the family I met in the lobby at my mechanic's. They were waiting for an oil change. They'd been part of the crowd waiting, stranded at the Superdome after the flood. A bus took them to Arkansas, where, "God bless them I know they were trying to be nice, but you do not put hot dogs in gumbo, even if it's just charity." They live in Little Rock now. They'd since bought a car, and came down for Carnival. The grandma had a big blue cooler sitting between her ankles. It was full of hot sausage to bring back. No more hot dogs in the gumbo.

I've taken fierce pride in being a local. Even if I was not born and raised here, New Orleans is where I grew up. When I do travel I'm a junky for talk about the city. Someone will ask, "So, how is it down there?" I launch into a litany. There are busted traffic lights, leaky sewer lines, mountains of debris, the skyrocketing murder rate, miles of desolation, and the levees still aren't fixed. "But you should come!" I say. It's like a battered beauty queen. Hard to look at, probably messed up even more on the inside than she is on the outside, but still regal and charming. This is where the listener I've taken hostage turns away slowly to engage someone less insane.

They don't understand that I'm in love. I talk to friends about New Orleans like a dysfunctional romance. I gush over it one day, then call up bawling and heartbroken the next. Why can't it change? Stop being self-destructive and violent? It has so much potential.

Recently, my blinders started to come off. It was building for awhile. My friend Helen Hill was murdered in her home. Other friends have been mugged. We don't go out much any more. Rarely on bikes.

But then there was this hot Friday night last month. I went on the perfect date with New Orleans. I went to a show, danced with friends on the stage, then headed home through my neighborhood of craftsman cottages and angel trumpets.

A block from my door, I was attacked from behind by a

stranger. He took my stuff, but after that there was a struggle. Shirt ripped off, his teeth sunk in my back. I escaped, with the help of my roommate. The case is moving forward, so I can't say much more than that.

Now I'm a jilted lover of the city. I'm angry and confused. Which is the real New Orleans? The one that's violent and desperate? Or the one that coos softly, and caresses me? The answer, of course, is both. But I just hauled my things out of New Orleans in a big truck.

2

I've had a hard time writing about New Orleans, though I think about it all the time. I'm in Los Angeles now, and there's no immediacy, no pressing reason to collect and organize thoughts about my old city. Don't think I'm moving back any time soon. The teeth marks on my back from the 19 (now 20, 21?) year-old who mugged and then attacked me have faded. He's serving several years in a Louisiana jail, though I don't know which one.

Out here, New Orleans never comes up in conversation organically. When people ask me about it, I assume they're being nice and making small talk, and I then feel resentful about their lack of sincerity over the city's plight. When people don't ask me about New Orleans, I feel compelled to bend their ears on it for a good, long bit as a kind of penance, or maybe punishment for not showing interest. Of course I'm being too hard on all these people, and on me.

On days when I tell myself I'm going to come home from my job and write something about New Orleans, I instead run a hot bath, watch my legs turn red in the water, and go to bed with a towel around me. I've signed a lease here. I've bought a couch that cost enough and would be hard enough to move that it must mean I've assigned some permanence to my situation. I live in a great neighborhood and I have many interesting, diverse friends.

At work I might Google Earth my old New Orleans street address. On the day the Googlers took the image, my roommate's Mardi Gras costume was still locked to the gas pipe out front. She turned a tandem bicycle into a rideable Indian elephant with chicken wire, gauzy gray fabric for the body, and glittery sequined mesh as a headdress and saddle. It became a landmark, a mascot really, for the whole block — her feat of arts and crafts, thrift and engineering. I hope coworkers will notice the elephant picture pulled up on my screen and ask what it is, because it sums up most of the things I love about my life in New Orleans.

They don't.

But in a way that's good. It means I don't have to get to the end of the story where I say that the glorious elephant bike was eventually stolen. The theft didn't happen until after I moved away, so in my mind I still see the elephant in the rearview mirror of a moving truck.

Also after I drove my stuff out of New Orleans: a girl had her throat slashed in the neighborhood bar where some of my closest friends spend maybe every other night. A family was killed in their New Orleans East home, childhood acquaintances of another friend of mine. That friend was mugged at gunpoint while getting into her car, by two teenagers who later that night got into a shootout with police at an abandoned housing project. My roommate's Vespa was stolen, later showed up on Craigslist, and she helped the police set up a sting to catch the thieves. Of course it was junked by the time they retrieved it. These things happened within a few months of my move.

About a year later after my move to L.A., my new boss

visits New Orleans for the first time. It's a five-day reporting trip in godawful July. She's wanted to go since Katrina. The third year anniversary is coming up at that point, and we've dedicated part of our radio show to it. I help coordinate her trip, suggest people to interview, and of course restaurants and bars. When she gets back I hear almost everyone in the office come by and give her big kudos for spending so much time and effort on the issues of New Orleans. During production of the show I freak out when someone suggests a piece of bluegrass music to put under an interview about someone's Katrina memoir. I get my first on-the-job reprimand for going behind the producer's back to find music that will make sense. "That's not a good use of your time," she says.

A few weeks after Hurricane Gustav misses New Orleans, I get a call from my sister as I walk up to the office. My sister lives in San Francisco, and we're close, but not 7:30 AM Monday morning close. Something was wrong.

"A girl I know was killed in New Orleans. She was shot. They found her ... multiple times in the head." She sobbed too hard to talk. I only got a few more details. Kirsten Brydum was around my sister's age, in her mid-20s. They ran in the same circles in San Francisco. Kirsten had set off to travel around the country, seeing how far she could get on a budget of pretty much nothing. She was visiting New Orleans to check it out and maybe do some volunteer work.

No leads in her murder. No motive. My sister says: "Why does it even matter what she was doing? Who deserves to get shot in the head? Multiple times." She couldn't stop thinking about how scared Kirsten must have been, how awful her last moments. The police got the call about her around eight in the morning on a Friday. She'd last been seen riding a borrowed bike away from a bar where a brass band was playing, around one in the morning. The stamp from the club was still on her hand.

I worry about telling this story, because I don't know the point of it. I'm afraid the talk around it will inevitably descend into clichés and epithets posing as discussion. Naive white do-gooders. Teenage thugs. Punk girl on bike. Black dude in oversize white t-shirt.

I also see that facts become very important after a crime. With me, I kept the shirt that was ripped off of me in my freezer for months, just in case the police changed their mind and wanted it for a DNA sample of the suspect's saliva. A friend of mine recently wrote a letter to the New Orleans paper, outraged that the police didn't seem to care that he'd obtained call logs from his service provider after his cellphone was stolen. The numbers, he pointed out, could have been traced to help find the person who mugged and threatened to kill him, his wife and their visiting friend.

With Kirsten's murder I was obsessed with the bike she'd borrowed from friends. The police didn't recover it. Did she ride it *to* the no-man's land where her body was found? It's a desolate stretch of the Upper Ninth Ward, near the empty Florida housing projects. Comments under the newspaper story about her death suggested she was a liberal tourist from California, probably looking to tour Katrina damage. I wanted proof that she wasn't, that she'd been taken there either already dead or to be killed. I was so adamant that the image of my sister's friend as a deluded happy freak not be promulgated that I wrote to the San Francisco obituary writer to ask about this sentence he wrote:

"On Saturday, while cycling after midnight in New Orleans after spending Friday evening in a dance club, she was shot in the head and killed in an apparent robbery."

My email said: "Do you know that she was cycling while shot, and not abducted and then shot? They didn't find the bike."

He did not. He didn't mean to suggest that in his sentence construction, and he was sorry.

The whole reason I've finally taken the time to write any of this is that a newspaper reporter in New Orleans has asked me to talk to him for a story he's writing. It's about violence and how it impacts people's views of New Orleans (I think). I looked up recent work. He's been covering the murder of a bartender in the French Quarter, shot in the face after some teenager tried to mug her. Three suspects have been arrested and may stand trial as adults. She was thirty-nine, preparing to get married and move away from New Orleans.

I don't want to be this person. I don't want commentary on violence in New Orleans to be my "bag," what I'm called on to talk about in public. Because I don't know about it, really. I didn't grow up with it; I haven't seen as much of it as many New Orleanians have, much less people living in war zones. I don't want to bring up murder at dinner parties or know what it feels like to sit on a witness stand and stare down a person who is going to jail because of what he did to you and your friend.

Why doesn't the reporter ask My Attacker for an interview about violence in New Orleans?

My Attacker. So intimate, but it is what I call him in my head. I think of writing to him, My Attacker. I want to know what he was thinking, if he was thinking. Would he really have killed me, or is that just something you say when you're him?

I want to tell him that there is love in the world. I want to say that some people who knew about that big, human love, named Helen and Kirsten, have been killed. But their deaths don't lead me to want pain and punishment for My Attacker. I want a better life for him. All those names printed on the church of that one New Orleans preacher — you know the one who puts the names of all the murder victims up — maybe all of them knew about love, too. Maybe My Attacker has seen that sign, and he'll be able to relate to that. I worry that this is a silly thought, that it has attached to it ideas of redemption along the lines of a Hollywood movie about inner-city black kids and their brave English teacher. Or worse, I worry that I am seeking answers for the deaths of others in the one person I know who has committed violence and been apprehended, like he's some lab specimen to be studied.

I worry more often about New Orleans becoming some dangerous and interesting footnote in my otherwise safe and upwardly mobile life.

I don't know how violence has affected my view of the city. I want to give the name of My Attacker to the reporter. In exchange for my comments, I want him to help me find out which prison he's in. I'll tell the reporter that tomorrow, and I'll let him make something out of what else I have to say.

Claudine came calling on a hot August night. Skinny, loud and a fetching tabby orange, she wandered off the street and onto our front porch, mewing insistently for food. In the coming weeks we would joke that someone should oil her. We called her Squeaky. We called her Eenie-Beenie. (She was both.) Two weeks later, we packed her into the car along with the two other cats, some of Greg's instruments and my hard drives, and made off for Austin. Our windows boarded, our neighbors bid adieu, we joined the legions on I-10 crawling east and west, carrying, along with their select possessions, differing degrees of fear and dread.

Borrowed Time

EVE ABRAMS

Gustav was my first evacu-cation (my boyfriend Greg's coinage), and once we heard New Orleans was fine and our neighborhood had power, I eased into the vacation aspect of things. We ate tacos and swam in Barton Springs and watched Sarah Palin make snarky remarks on TV. We shot little Claudine full of vaccinations, and several days later, drove home, swapped stories and went back to life.

It was easy for me. Gustav unleashed no Katrina memories, no post traumatic stress or anxiety. I was still living in Brooklyn in 2005 — a lover of New Orleans, but not yet a resident of it. I watched the horror from a safe, outraged distance, making frantic calls to friends' cellphones, which never rang. But for those whose home was then New Orleans, Gustav was an emotional time machine. The week Gustav meandered to Louisiana (coincidentally, the week of Katrina's three year anniversary), the news was on in every room at work — first in the background, and eventually, the event all ears and eyes turned to. We leaned into desks and absorbed ominous terms like *cone* and *eye*. We calculated winds and rains and directions, and scrutinized experts, and offered our own analyses. I heard it over and over again: *if this one is like Katrina, I am not coming back. I can't do that again.*

I REMEMBER THE PIVOT POINT: a sunny January day in 2006. I was sweeping the kitchen floor in my Brooklyn apartment. The radio was on, and a woman on NPR made a plea: if you care about New Orleans, go there for Mardi Gras. I stopped mid-stroke, and my eyes went from the plants in my south-facing window, bathed in a bright sea of winter light, to the five framed photographs hanging on the wall behind me — of trees and shadows and Creole cottages — suffused in a different kind of light: New Orleans in April at dusk. This woman, this voice on the radio, of course she was talking to me. Who else would she be talking to?

I called Ann Marie, who hadn't moved back yet, but whose sister Monique had. I called Chris, who was working in Shreveport but would be back in New Orleans for Mardi Gras. I cobbled together places to stay and booked a flight, and not long after, I was riding in a cab down Dauphine Street. It was Thursday morning, hours before Muses would roll, hours before I would dress as a pirate and exclaim "Aargh" as a means of communication. At Monique's house at last, a cute boy, fresh from sleep, answered the door. His name was Greg.

THIS THAT I AM WRITING is not a love story, but I love my boyfriend very much. It is convenient for me that the man I love also loves New Orleans, for it is him who finally got me here, away from the land of work-too-much and connect-too-little. Five years passed between my meeting New Orleans and my moving to New Orleans, and in those five years, we nearly lost her. Yes, she changed, but New Orleans is still the closest thing we have to New Orleans.

Before I moved, when I still lived in Brooklyn and realized I was moving, what scared me wasn't New Orleans' weather or water levels or even its violence. What scared me was the years passing, with New Orleans still being New Orleans, and me *not* being there. Me missing that. What scared me was the inability to make up for what I did not do, for the time squandered, for the time which is now, which is all we have.

HERE ON SAINT CLAUDE AVENUE, Greg and I live in one half of a double shotgun with three cats: Sabrina, Sunshine and Claudine, otherwise known as Eenie-Beenie. Of the five of us, Claudine is the only one from here. Sabrina (the foul natured but charming cat) and Sunshine (the mentally challenged, frightened cat) — are from New York. As is Greg, though he is from Central New York, not Brooklyn. I am from Maryland, by way of New York, and when I am being thorough, I answer the question that way.

But Eenie-Beenie is from here, a native, a true New Orleanian. She bounds through the backyard, amid her native grasses, around her native trees, killing native rodents, frolicking in native ways. She hides behind the banana tree and romps through the wild asparagus. The lead levels in our soil are frighteningly, dangerously high, and so our lettuce and mustard greens and basil are in elevated beds filled with store bought soil, and Claudine dashes between these too. She circles and pounces and turns on a dime, running in one direction and then the next. For a few moments at a time, she sits on my lap as I swing in the hammock Greg bought me for my birthday, and then she leaps off in pursuit of something. Lucky girl. This is the only home she's ever known.

Undoubtedly my accent gives me away, my mid-Atlantic blankness. I'm fairly textbook in my execution of the English language — a shame in this land of eccentric elocution, where inflections vary with the crossing of a street or generation. I pronounce my r's like r's (rather than oi's, rather than not pronouncing them at all), and I speak quickly, without a lilt. (I am, however, becoming rather fond of saying "baby.") People ask all the time where I'm *from*, despite the local doctrine that it's the mix which matters.

We hear a lot about the *gumbo* here in New Orleans, the French-African-Spanish-Native American-American-Caribbean-Creole-Italian-German-what-have-you mix. In this metaphor, New Orleans is the bowl which holds the parts, and I am an ingredient dunked in it. An older gentleman of the sort who pronounces *New Orleans* using a minimum of four syllables, whose family meandered here circa the Louisiana Purchase, told me recently that it's the people from elsewhere who care most about preserving the city. Born of other lands, he posited, we most appreciate the uniqueness of this place. We know how different New Orleans is from the land of stripmallconcrete. We value the music in the streets, as well as the oaks and palms at their borders. We work to keep it *it*. I like hearing I'm of use, especially from a former King of Carnival.

There's no denying the power of the mix. The yield is noteworthy: Jazz, French Quarter buildings, Vietnamese poboys, Mardi Gras Indians (to name but a few). Even more important is the message of the mix: you too can be part of this place; New Orleans is here to accept you. In other words, if you understand the need to eat and parade and congregate and play and listen and sing, space will be made for your particular way of doing these things. We will not be surprised by your outfit. We will not tell you to lower your voice. We will call you whatever name you declare, whether it be Shaggy or Firefly or Junior or Dookey. In New Orleans you get to be who you say you are. Names mythic or fanciful or normal, names which appeared on nary a birth certificate, appear here and form identities both familiar and absurd. My declarations have been conventional, but transformative nonetheless. I've said "writer" and "radio producer," and voila, I am.

Claudine, the night she appeared, said the same thing over and over again, and transform her life it did. I brought her food, and moments later, I brought her inside. Greg told me to get her out, but instead I gave her a flea bath, and put her on the back porch inside one of our cat carriers, with more food and water. Greg made mild protestations, and I ignored them. The next day, when I called home from work, Greg told me he'd made her a bed in the bathroom and that he'd named her Claudine. Despite the obvious correlation of "Claudine" to the street she wandered in from, it took me months to understand the connection. Thank goodness. Apparently the other contestant was Claudette.

We tried to find space in a no-kill shelter. We took ridiculously cute pictures and sent them to friends. We listed her many charms: incessant purring, fuzzy orange appearance. But no one took her, and each day we loved her more. Then we evacuated, and somewhere between Louisiana and Texas and Louisiana, she became ours.

IN A FEW MONTHS, THE weather will turn subtropical again. Sabrina and Sunshine will begin their summer activities: laying around in earnest. On the wooden floor boards and under the tub and in whatever room the air conditioner is turned on, they will be supine and immobile for hours, days, months. Meanwhile, at a point unknown in the endlessness of summer, Eenie-Beenie will pass the one year mark and officially leave kittenhood behind. What will become of her zip zapping about, her bullet-like sprints across the lawn? Will young Claudine begin to show the maturity of her age?

It's impossible to know, for New Orleans moves at such iconoclastic speeds. It's hard to miss how s–l–o–w life can be here, how utterly uninterested we are in efficiency and expediency.[1] But equally amazing is how fast life is. Hanging above my desk is a photograph of our house taken right after the storm — when it was just Greg's house, before it was mine too. The gingerbread is slightly less grey than the rest of it, and between the shuttered shutters is a message spray painted in black by lord knows who, quoting either James Baldwin or the bible: "FIRE the NEXT time." It's a color photograph, but you have to look hard to know it: the scattering of weeds at the very bottom, tussling between the two stoops, are green, not grey.

Underneath this photograph is another one, taken by the same photographer, from the same angle, a year and a half later. The house has been painted a Caribbean green with yellow trim. Gone is the spray painted note of cataclysmic abandon, and in the foreground, where once there were weeds, are the

---

1 Why, for example, bother to have more than one bank teller deal with a line of fifteen people? Why change into the other absolutely *empty* lane next to you and drive on, when you can sit behind an unmoving car — which, lack of turn signal aside, appears to be making a left — and wait until it is no longer in your path?

young oleander, crepe myrtle, and Mexican palm trees we'd recently planted. The only thing *not* bursting with color is the sky — a bland white, just like in the photograph above it.

So different are these two images of this same place, they look as if they were snapped in different decades. But it's a year and a half that separates them. If you took that same shot today, the oleander and palm would tower in front of the house, obscuring the grillwork on the porch. So too the willow we planted a year after that, which climbed ten feet up and wept abundantly down, showering the strip of grass between sidewalk and street with wispy fronds of delicate green. Expanding boundlessly, blossoming in every direction, these trees are the definition of lush. From nothing to lush, in less than two years. If this isn't fast, what is?

It's the sun and the rain, of course. Nature's steroids. Leave during the summer, even for a few weeks, and you risk returning to a jungle. We have a bush in the back, a weed tree with lovely yellow flowers, which doggedly loves life. It easily quadruples in size every several months, pushing out branches in every conceivable direction, taking up as much of the yard as you allow it. Along with shutters for the windows, New Orleans homes should come with machetes.

The star of our plant show is the Mexican palm, robustly unfolding its spiky, deep green self in perfect (and eventually ragged) fans. We almost didn't buy it. The man at Bantings, the walking-plant-encyclopedia-man, warned us that in 30 years, the palm could grow so big that it might upset the sidewalk, or the electrical wires, or even the house. But I reasoned that we didn't know if New Orleans would be around in 30 years, that in all likelihood, the Gulf waves would by then be lapping at our levees, working to subside even this land where we live: the high ground, New Orleans' treasured sliver by the river. Greg told me I was terrible for saying such things. But I am a realist, on top of a dreamer.

It is hard to explain this dichotomous way of living— the planting of a garden, the building of a career, the investment of time, money, and love in a place you are thoroughly unsure will survive. But you only think this way when you think about it, which you generally only do during hurricane season. The rest of the year you don't remember to consider such things. You forget about the articles and books you've read — about wetlands and sea level rise. You don't notice the puddles on the neutral ground or in the backyard, forming in the rain but staying around long after. The tires of your car, like donuts dunked in coffee: you don't notice these either. You put a bag over your head. It's the same bag you wear when you buy something cheap which says "Made in China," or when you eat chicken from a factory, or when you drive your car to the gym rather than bike the mile on flat, sunny streets. This is living in New Orleans, or maybe it's living in America, and in either case, this is where I live.

But just to be on the safe side, we planted the palm next to the curb, rather than the house. You never know. We (our state and country *we*) might get smart and do something. Or perhaps the disappearance of our delta will take longer than the current statistical trajectory suggests (a whopping 24 square miles of wetlands are lost per year — subsided or eroded out to sea). [2] Maybe science, or god, will come to the rescue. In any case, we're renters. We won't be living here, in this house, in thirty years.

Before I moved from that other sea level city, up North, I thought about these things, and I decided I'd squandered thirty odd years not living in New Orleans. Now I wanted her, for as long as I could have her. Life is borrowed time anyway,

2   Louisiana Department of Natural Resources

no matter where you are or what you do. We get a handful of decades, and for the most part, I've been lucky enough to choose where I spend them.

For now, until I can't, I choose here: where the air smells of trumpet flowers and jasmine, where I feel beautiful and lucky to be alive, where schizophrenics and boys with instruments and people with plastic cups roam the streets, where I know and love my neighbors and my hair gets frizzy fast, where the universe is made of stories (thank you Muriel Rukeyser), not atoms, and where everything is seeped in layers — strata of dirt and plants and time and lineage. I choose New Orleans, where life is thick with living. Call out your food metaphors! Your images of swamp, bayou, and roux! I pick this perilous, faulty place. Because I love it, and what better reason is there?

Eenie-Beenie won't live to see the palm imperil the house, the city saved or submerged. Cats get less time. They don't generally make it past twenty, and if Claudine lives that long, romping and then ambling through this green, hot, pain in the arse paradise, I'll consider myself, and her, quite lucky. She'll be one of those New Orleanians we read about, the kind born and bred here, the kind who tend not to go anywhere else, at least not for very long. And even when she's old and grown, even when it's no longer remotely true, I'll still call her Eenie-Beenie, because that's her name now, and that's how we do things here.

Monday night was beautiful, man.

When I saw all my brothers and sisters (and seesters) in that crowd Monday, I knew we were back. Not just the Saints back in NOLA, back in the dome.

The city was going to come back.

An entire group 69,503 people (Atlanta got 500 tickets) that you don't have to *explain* New Orleans to. A group of people that *get* po-boys, that *get* second lines, that *get* Carnival, that *get* red beans and rice with sausage on a Monday night, that *get* lagniappe, that *get* "gimme an amber," that *will call you* honey and darlin', that know home depot like the back of their hand, that can hang drywall in their sleep, that can recommend the best mask for dust and the best mask for stink-mold, that can tell you where to get your flat fixed, that think both gravy and mayo on a sandwich is a good thing, that party Saturday night and go to church Sunday morning and leave the service in time for kickoff, that go to Vaughn's on Thursday nights, that know the game wasn't rigged, that think we are going to the playoffs, that believe that Buddy D and Vera and Sam Mills were watching from up above and toasting the return of our Saints to their rightful home.

It ain't over until you hug the ushers on your way out of the dome.

It ain't over until you fire up the big ass cuban cigar.

It ain't over until your ears quit ringing (Tuesday at about 3:30 in the afternoon).

This is not a sports blog, this is a *New Orleans* blog. I care about 2 things: my family and my city, and last weekend I was looking at real estate in the Chicago metro area, because my love for the former makes me consider leaving the latter. It would be so much easier for me to live there. I wouldn't have to worry about school districts or mold or my outrageous power bills or my depression or the cracks in my walls or evacuation routes or day care or doctors moving away or universities closing departments or hospitals shutting down or random bullets.

But then, I wouldn't have to worry about living in a city with a soul, either.

Once again, New Orleans is the only city that ever loved me back. When I was in the dome, I knew why: *our people.*

Ashley Morris, Sept. 27, 2006

"Calhoun Superette," the Professor said. No hello, no introduction. Phone rang and he cut right to the chase.

"What?"

"Poor boys. It's too late for coffee, let's get us some poor boys at the Superette and take 'em back to my place."

The Professor had one of his rare weekdays in New Orleans. It was semester break, late December, and so he didn't have to fly back to his teaching gig in Chicago until after the holiday. We'd planned on coffee, but he was getting his glasses fixed and I had conference calls all morning, so breakfast had turned into lunch, and lunch, in New Orleans, requires negotiations.

In My Home Over There

RAY SHEA

"Dude, I'm tired of the Superette. I've been eating there non-stop since Guy's closed after the fire. Besides, I need to get farther away from the neighborhood. I'm going stir crazy up here." I loved the Superette, most underrated roast beef poor boy in town, but you can burn out on even the best every once in a while, and working from home you tended to wear out the places within a one-mile radius.

"Well, I've been to Parkway twice this week," the Professor said, "so that's out."

I sighed, and idly poked around on my laptop, my finger

memory automatically cycling through email, Facebook, couple of blogs, my eyes not taking in any of it. Waiting for lunch inspiration.

The Professor was persistent. "Domilise's?"

"Nah, I think they're closed Mondays these days."

"I thought they were closed Tuesdays."

"I can never remember. Anyway, I hate driving all the way over there and finding out they're closed."

"Ray, man, this is fucking New Orleans, are you honestly trying to tell me you're stuck in a food rut?"

"Well I'm not exactly dressed for Galatoire's, y'know. I telecommute. You're lucky I'm not naked."

"Stop it, you'll ruin my appetite."

Silence. We both pondered. And then inspiration flew in on battered wings.

"Chicken!" I said.

You could hear the Professor's ears perking up even over the shitty T-Mobile connection. "Chicken?"

"Definitely chicken. Willie Mae's Scotch House is re-opened now. Let's go down and get us some local culture."

"Done and done. See you in five."

NINETY SECONDS LATER I WAS riding shotgun in the Professor's minivan. I had to clear away a juice box and some ancient French fries to make room; the Professor had a brood of three preschoolers at home, so his van had the eternal crust of snacks eaten on the road.

"Ah, toddler droppings. I remember those days. Don't miss 'em."

The Professor cackled. "Uh-huh. How's the whole 13-going-on-17 thing working out with your daughter?"

"Shut up. Asshole. Talk to me in ten years and see if you

think it's so fucking funny."

"You have my sympathy. God forbid she meet any guys like us."

"Noooo shit."

"So you been to Willie Mae's since they opened?"

"No, but I saw the movie about her at the film festival last month. You see that?" The Professor looked over his shoulder turning onto Carrollton, then shook his head. "Heard about it."

"So Willie Mae, she's in exile after the storm in Houston with her family, and disappears," I said. "This is when the city is still closed, roadblocks everywhere, y'know? A few days later, some EMT is wandering through the Treme, and there's Willie Mae sitting on the steps of her restaurant looking lost. Says she came back to clean up and get the place opened. Eighty-five fucking years old, the only person around for a mile, and all she had was her purse with an MRE and her James Beard medal in it. Nobody even knows how she got from Houston to New Orleans, never mind how she managed to sneak into the city."

"Shit, she should give lessons to FEMA. Federal government couldn't even find us on a map and old ladies are just walking here from Houston."

"No kidding. Nothing gets done here you don't do it yourself, even if you're an old lady who makes chicken."

"Damn good chicken."

"I don't think I'd want chicken from FEMA."

"Probably have formaldehyde in it, like their trailers."

"Anyway, the place needed so much work and took so long to remodel she doesn't even want it any more. You know she tried to sell it to Lolis Elie on the first day?" Elie was a local journalist and filmmaker.

"Serious?"

"Yeah, they got footage of it in the movie. She was tired."

"The fucking storm really messed up the old people."

"Messed everybody up. I didn't even live here for the storm and it's messing me up. I'm medicated out the wazoo." The Professor and I were both New Orleans expats who came back after the storm. Some misguided sense of civic pride mixed with homesickness, I guess. A few people thought we were heroes. The rest of them thought we were nuts. I tended to subscribe to the nut theory.

You could see the progress along the main avenues as we drove through Mid-City. New restaurants opened up, old ones restored. Venezia, Brocato's. Then a whole block of boarded up houses with search-and-rescue markings on the doors, the fading brown smudge of the high-water-mark bathtub ring stretching down the block from house to house, straight as a carpenter's level. Then a shiny new coffee shop.

We turned down Orleans Avenue, past the American Can Company building. An old cannery from the city's manufacturing heyday, it had long been converted to condos before Katrina struck. The ensuing battle of the Can Company is legend now: surrounded by eleven-foot-deep flood waters, some Desert Storm vets who lived there turned it into a fortress and refuge for hundreds of neighborhood residents, protecting them from looters and thugs, and organizing foraging parties for food and water. Watching day after day as helicopters flew back and forth ignoring their rooftop signs pleading for rescue.

The ground floor shops were all open again. A couple of NOPD cops stood on the steps shooting the shit and sipping lattes. No sign of the battle of the cannery. Just another mixed-use development, condos with a waterfront view.

The Professor was trying to navigate. "Where do I turn?"

"I don't remember. It's on St. Ann and something-something. I don't remember if it's one-way or not."

"I think it is. We'll drive as far as Dooky Chase's and then cut over and double back."

"Too bad Dooky's is still closed. I've still never eaten there."

"You've never eaten at Dooky Chase's? Are you nuts?"

"Hey, man, I moved away when I was twenty. I couldn't afford it back then, and it ain't been open since I got back."

We passed down Orleans, the Lafitte Projects on our right, Dooky's on the left.

With a big "OPEN" sign taped to the door.

Five minutes later, we were inside Dooky Chase's at the counter.

"Hey, baby, how you doin'? We open, but only to go."

"Fine with me," the Professor said. "Food's still good, right?"

"Oh, yeah, it's good."

I took a look at the take-out menu. "How much chicken can you eat?"

"All of it," the Professor said.

"Indeed."

He scanned the menu and leaned over to me.

"I'll have four fried chickens, and a Coke."

"And some dry white toast, please."

"I like a man who knows his Blues Brothers."

"Indeed. No Aretha Franklin here though."

"Leah Chase is cooler than Aretha Franklin."

"I wonder if she's here."

The counter girl was waiting with her pen. "She in back. Y'all know what you wanna order?"

We decided to split a whole fried chicken and four sides. One order of yams, because I have to have yams. One order of greens, because our mamas would want us to eat our veggies. And two orders of mac'n'cheese, because we knew we wouldn't be able to share a single order of the mac without somebody getting hurt. And two Barqs in bottles to drink at the brand new mahogany bar while we waited.

I wondered aloud where we were going to eat all this food.

"I suppose we could lug it all back home and eat it."

"Nah," countered the Professor. "We should eat it while it's hot."

"The Quarter is closer. Maybe Jackson Square or the levee by the Moonwalk?"

The Professor took a swig of his Barq's and shrugged.

We sat in silence, working our root beers, looking at the original art on the walls — an oil painting of Louis Armstrong, a black-and-white photo of an old jazz funeral — 'til our food was ready and we found ourselves standing outside on the doorstep, feast in hand and no place to go.

It was one of those gray December days right before Christmas where it hadn't made up its mind whether to be warm and wet or cold and wet until right that moment, and apparently cold and wet was winning. A slight mist was desperately trying to grow up to be a light drizzle. The French Quarter seemed like half a city away, our warm houses even farther, and our stomachs were churning at the smell of the chicken wafting out of the plastic bags in our hands.

"Well," I said, half-joking, "we could always just go eat at the projects."

"Dude."

Directly across Orleans Avenue, sealed up, silent and desolate, stood the historic Lafitte Housing Projects. Built in the early 1940s as the African-American alternative to the then-white Iberville projects, Lafitte was not your typical public housing. The sturdy brick buildings faced onto grassy tree-shaded courtyards and looked to my eyes like one of the student residential quads where I went to college. But soon after Katrina, suspiciously soon in fact, city and federal agencies swooped in and sealed up the entire complex, locking out the mostly working-class and working-poor residents who were trying to return home. The fate of Lafitte had already been decided by bureaucrats long ago. They would soon be torn down.

"Dude, we have to do this," I said.

"A farewell meal for Lafitte? Hell yeah."

We lugged our loot across the street, through traffic, and past the "No Trespassing" signs, getting odd looks here and there from passersby, until we found ourselves the perfect front porch on which to spread our picnic lunch. Conversation stopped while we tore into the chicken.

"Jesus, this is good."

"Mmmph."

"They got any napkins in that bag? I got chicken all over me."

"Mmmph."

I broke into the yams.

"Oooooooh. I can't believe they call this a vegetable. This tastes like goddamn bread pudding. Here, you have to try this."

"Save me half, I'm working on some mac."

"Oh, hey, hand me one o' them."

I took my mac'n'cheese and a fork and wandered out into the grass, avoiding the marshy bits where the ground looked like it never really drained right, and turned to look back at the building.

"So you know what's weird about this?"

The Professor tore some skin off a drumstick. "What's that?"

"All the doors and windows are all sealed up with these

metal plates that are bolted on. Metal plates that fix exactly into each opening, like they were designed for it."

"Huh. That is strange."

"I mean, this place has, what, eight or nine hundred apartments? Probably several thousand windows and doors? So right at the same time that the government couldn't even get food and water down here, somebody managed to schlep up several thousand pre-fitted industrial-strength covers to seal up the entire project. It's almost like this stuff was all ready to go in some warehouse somewhere, just waiting for the right moment."

"It's called disaster capitalism, man. They have this stuff all planned out in advance. You think they wrote the Patriot Act in response to 9/11? Fuck, man, that shit was sitting in Karl Rove's top drawer for years waiting for an opportunity, and on 9/12 he whipped it out and started sending copies around to his buddies."

"I hear people's stuff is still inside these apartments. They just sealed it all up while everybody was stuck in Houston. Clothes, furniture, toys, refrigerators and all. I can't believe they can get away with that."

"They can do whatever they want. They *are* doing whatever they want."

"But it makes no sense. I mean, look at the high water mark on that building. It's barely at the level of the first floor. This unit might not even have flooded. It shouldn't take anything to rehab this place. Fuck, my brother got four feet of water in Metairie and he was back in his house within a year."

"Dude, they don't want them back. What better way to whiten up a city than destroy all the places black people live?"

"Yeah, like New Orleans doesn't need these people back. They work. How you gonna run a tourist economy with no cab drivers or cooks or dishwashers or truck drivers?"

"Or musicians. I hear half of the Soul Rebels still have to commute from Houston to play gigs here 'cause they have no place to live. And they play all the time."

I shook my head while I dug at the bottom of the mac'n'cheese. "Damn, that was good."

"Here, you want the rest of these yams?"

"Why, you don't want 'em? That's your half."

"They're my last gift to you."

"What, you leaving soon?"

"Fuck no, I'm not going anywhere. This is just the last time I give away food to you."

"Awright, you say so. You're missing out."

The Professor licked the last of the chicken off his fingers and lay back on the concrete steps.

"Man. This is it. This is why I am here."

"Serious. You know something? We're standing here in the cold, in the rain, in an abandoned and condemned housing project, eating Creole soul food out of a cardboard container, getting dirty looks from passersby, and what are we thinking? That this is the fucking life. This is how we want to live."

"That's *it*, man. This is New Orleans. This is why people in America don't get us. This is why they hate us so much. Because they have no fucking comprehension of how fantastic this is."

"Exactly!"

"Fuck, this is not just lunch for us. This is life. You know what they're eating in Houston right now? Fucking Quizno's that they bought in a drive-through. And they *like* it. They're idiots."

I scraped the last shred of sugary yams and yammy sugar from the corners of the Styrofoam cup and sat back down next to the Professor.

"So how long you think you'll be able to keep commuting

to Chicago every week?"

"Hell, I don't know, man," he said. "It's exhausting. Fucking utilities are raping us. House costs a fortune, but I gotta stay in that neighborhood 'cause of the school."

"Yeah, I know the feeling."

"Tranked to the tits just to stay sane."

"Oh, same, same."

"Better to live here in sackcloth and ashes than to own the entire shitty stink-hole of Chicago though."

"Indeed, indeed."

And we sat there on the steps, happy in the moment. Happy to be alive, at this very place, at this very point in history, feeling like every meal, every party, every chance conversation was fraught with import.

"Gentlemen, if I could please have you line up on either side, facing the casket. Honorary pallbearers, if you could please step to the rear."

I looked down at the narrow silver rail near my hands. Narrow because the casket was so large, the maximum that would fit in the mausoleum space purchased just days before. I wiped my sweaty palm on my suit pants. How would I be able to do this? I felt nothing. No sadness, no fear, no relief. Just empty. I looked up, across the casket at Mark. He was looking down at his hands, ashen-faced. I wondered if he worried about lifting it.

"OK, both hands on the rail in front of you, please, gentlemen. On three we're going to lift him and take him out the door and down three steps to the hearse. All right, gentlemen, one, two, three."

I lifted. Somebody behind me grunted. He was so much heavier than my grandmother had been.

"Now forward, please. Both hands, now! Watch the door

frame behind you."

We awkwardly shuffled sideways toward the steps, bearing the big guy. The hearse waited at the bottom, doors yawning wide, all chrome wheels and hardware where we would set him down …

IT WAS STARTING TO RAIN HARDER.

"Should we be getting back? I got a conference call at two. The bosses in Austin aren't really hip to the slow pace of life here, so I need to get back to keep up appearances."

"Yeah, I need to pick up the girl from preschool."

We packed the trash up in the plastic bags and headed back across the street to the parking lot. The local Fox affiliate was filming something at the front door of Dooky's.

"You think they got any footage of us?"

"Ha! 'What were these fat white men doing in the projects today at lunchtime? We'll have the story at ten. Plus Bob Breck on your Weather Authority, Fox 8.'"

"Fuck Bob Breck. They should bring Nash out of cryogenic storage."

"They will when hurricane season starts back up. Can't have a hurricane without Nash."

I walked in a fog, parked cars and above-ground mausoleums on my left, the hearse moving at a crawl on my right. Around us girls in roller skates and black angel's wings skated in circles, but I took no joy in it. The big guy was married to a roller derby skater. He'd wanted a jazz funeral; I don't think he ever imagined he'd get full military honors from the derby league too.

I didn't know how to walk. Tried the half step gait I'd seen old black men do at jazz funerals, but I kept falling behind the front wheel of the hearse, so I just walked. What was appropriate?

What did it matter? The big guy was dead, and I never got to say goodbye, and I never had time to be sad. There is always so much to do when somebody dies, and you find time to do it all, and then you wonder why you never managed to find all that time to spend together when he was alive.

So I walked, on a bright sunny day in the gray fog, feeling nothing, seeing up ahead the Hot 8 Brass Band in funeral black and white, preceding the hearse on the trek to the final resting place, the funeral dirge not penetrating the mist of numbness enveloping my mind …

WE WERE ALMOST HOME.

"Which street do I turn on, Jeannette?"

"Nah, keep going," I pointed. "Go up to Plum Street and turn left, then you gotta come back up, it's all one-way streets."

"So you staying for Christmas?"

"No, it's the in-laws turn this year, so I'll be in a gated compound in a gated community outside a suburb of a suburb of Fort Worth."

"Oh, joy."

"Yeah, pretty much God's country out there, but they make you feel at home, and I get to eat pie breakfast, lunch, and dinner."

"Lemme know when you get back, we'll do Willie Mae's."

"Mos' def. We need to hit Li'l Dizzy's too. And I wanna go out some night, maybe see Rebirth at the Maple Leaf."

"That can easily be arranged, my friend."

A trombone smear broke the fog open, "The Old Rugged Cross" no longer a funeral dirge, now this is New Or-LEANS, music, y'all, and for the first time I felt the sun on my face, and I smiled a little smile. And then a big smile, and then I wondered if it was unseemly for a pallbearer to grin like an idiot while marching alongside the hearse, and I looked across the hood of the car at John who was leading the bearers on the other side. He had his sunglasses on, his hands folded in front of him, a beatific smile of his own raised to the sun, and I could tell he was feeling that trombone like I was ...

"SO TELL YOUR BOY HE needs to come over some time so I can take slap shots at him. We need to toughen him up if he's gonna play goalie for the twelve-year-olds next year." The Professor was always up for a little hockey brutality.

"Will do. He's also asking when you're gonna come over and give him a drum lesson. I think he wants to learn some street beats. He's already bummed 'cause I told him he's not going to be going to St. Aug for high school."

"Yeah, well, maybe we can inject some funky marching tradition into Lusher somehow."

"Ha! Yeah, right."

"OK, later, homes."

"See ya."

I swung the door shut and the Professor drove off into the drizzle, him to his home life, leaving me to mine. And for a while New Orleans retreated as I buried myself back in the increasingly alien world of my remote high-tech employer in Austin, where two-hour soul food lunches in the rain are an alien concept.

"Ray," somebody whispered, "put your lapel flower on the casket."

I fumbled with the pin, but my fingers were shaking too much, so he helped me unclasp it, pull the flower from the pin and toss it onto the box, on top of the Saints flag draped across the top. I didn't know what to do with the pin. I kept trying to put it in the breast pocket of my suit, but it was a faux pocket, and as the minister delivered the final prayer, the wind kicked up so that we all had to put one hand down to keep the flag from blowing away. I fumbled and fumbled with the damn pin until I finally dropped it on the ground.

The prayer concluded, and I did not see the signal but some-how the band knew to start, not a dirge this time, but something soulful, maybe Marvin Gaye, something to take us out and away from the grave, back into the light, into the world of the living, where people still danced and ate and drank, where a city still thrived, still struggled and grew despite the continual losses and injuries and insults that piled up higher than the storm debris that used to line the streets.

The big guy was gone, but the big guy would never leave New Orleans again.

I took my hand from the casket for the last time. The flag did not blow away.

THE PROFESSOR DIED IN APRIL, all alone in a hotel room in another state. He came home in a slate-blue, extra-large casket and was brought to rest per his instructions at St. Louis Cemetery #3, a stone's throw from Jazz Fest, with the Hot 8 Brass Band and dozens of roller girls and hundreds of friends and several busloads of perplexed tourists in attendance. He was gone, but he was also home.

In May, I was driving up Orleans Avenue and happened to see a giant backhoe knocking down the very building at Lafitte where we'd eaten lunch that December day. A week later there was nothing left but a flat, empty lot. The people who lived there? I don't know if they will ever be home.

c

When my work on earth is done,
At the setting of life's sun,
I am going to my home over there.
I will walk the golden stair,
And be free from every care,
I'll be a-happy in my home over there.

"In My Home Over There,"
MAHALIA JACKSON
(Music by Rev. B.W. Smith)
1947

Sometimes, when the sunset fires up the Creole colors of the houses just right, I'm able to see New Orleans with a long view. A future nostalgia travels across time and gathers like a good afternoon rain cloud in my heart, washing a supreme sadness over me. *There will come a time when you don't live here,* it says, *and this — this very moment — is what you'll remember.*

This is the beauty of New Orleans.

For Now

ALI ARNOLD

New Orleanians find few reasons to cross a bridge because we can move through time and space just by standing still on the corner, listening to God himself stroll into the streets on the notes of a horn that trills into the night. The people follow, spilling out onto the sidewalk, a subtle (and sometimes outright) dance in their hips as they sway to the music that leads us all to that space between here and there, now and then.

Some of my relatives who live just below the buckle of the Bible Belt continue to ask me why I don't "come home," how I can tolerate living in "that city of sin," the present day Sodom and Gomorrah. But I find the reverse to be true: New Orleans is one of the few places where people are ever searching for that transcendent experience that reminds us of all that is pure and absolute. Sure, maybe some people are searching in the wrong places, but I would rather live among people who are looking, who have open eyes and often, open hearts, and who honor death by celebrating life.

THE FEW MONTHS BEFORE KATRINA — and yes, I must bring her up, because she's become a locus, in a strange way, marking that spot in time when our entire worlds shifted — so yes, in the few months before Katrina, I had been away, far away in Prague, the city of spires. There, the people I passed in the street never acknowledged my presence, so when I walked out of my shotgun in the Bywater on that first morning back in the city that care forgot and was greeted with a "Good Morning" from a fellow I'd never seen before, I bent over and kissed the sidewalk. My love for this place welled up inside me and spilled over onto the street corner, yet again. If I'd known then that just a few days later, I'd be whisked away for another three months, I might have said more than Thanks, God, for New Orleans.

In those early days after Katrina, it seemed that everybody was grateful for this place. Somehow, it didn't matter that the electricity was off as much it was on, that we were repairing tires routinely (having run over roofing nails in the street), or that we were searching daily for a store that had potable water in stock ("potable" having become a new addition to our vernacular). We were still proud and excited to be here, to be home. Almost immediately, everyone had a sticker, expressing their love for our crescent city. "Be a New Orleanian wherever you are" was one of the first I saw (and proudly donned, I might add). Later, "New Orleans: Proud to Swim Home," a clever redux on the pre-Katrina "New Orleans: Proud to Call it Home." The sticker mottos quickly moved onto t-shirts, and suddenly, the tourist trap shops in the Quarter were challenged by several burgeoning t-shirt storefronts selling local pridewear. My favorites were the ones that simply read "By-water" or "Uptown" or "Mid-City," allowing us the opportunity to advertise that we were replanting ourselves in our communities, with even deeper roots than before.

Despite this growing love for our city, many of us who lived in New Orleans before the storm were surprised that so many people moved to NOLA afterwards. Even though we had a sense that we were living in a historic moment, a moment we treasured, we couldn't help but wonder about these newcomers. What were their motivations? Why now? Perhaps these people looked down their streets one night during sunset and caught a long view of their own lives and thought, *There may come a time when New Orleans may not be there.* Perhaps a sadness flooded their hearts at the thought, and so they crossed a bridge and moved into our little fishbowl, where the streets fill with water when it rains, where the termites swarm in the spring right before the stinging caterpillars appear in droves, where we may be halfway through Revelation, but, by God, we're still kicking and in time with the music, too.

SO, NOW, HERE WE ALL are, New Orleanians by birth or by choice, sitting on our stoops, watching the sun set and listening to the music of our city, a testimony to its endurance and vitality. The cicadas make their own music, competing with so many others — the calliope whistling on the river, the hum of the Quarter which changes pitch but never ceases, the laughter of a neighbor who stirs up a bit a fun even in this soupy heat, and yes, the horns which always make their way out of the corner club to induce a bit of strutting and stepping on the street. We listen to the space between the notes of this jazz happening all around us, this jazz that is our city. We wipe the sweat from our foreheads, take another long, cold drink, and wonder if any other place makes a music that can compete with the beauty of our city's song.

And then, as if we swallowed it, there it is, that future nostalgia. In this moment, everything shifts. The air gets lighter but the colors become more saturated, and we feel the weight of the recognition that beneath the street is the beach. This long view of time washes over us, and we yearn to be like the sand and simply shift under the water, swaying in time to the rhythm of the waves. We silently acknowledge that there may come a time when we're not here, but we're here now. Rather than fight the current, we'll commune with it instead. We'll drink it in and sweat it out and lift our glasses in gratitude. For now.

Eve Shoshanah Abrams rarely uses her middle name. She has three cats and a fiancé and far too many clothes. She buys her food at the Farmer's Market. She used to live in Brooklyn, but now she lives on St. Claude Avenue, her command center for producing radio stories, writing and doing all manner of things.

husband, in 1857-1858, and made a connection between slavery and the subservient state of women. One newspaper wrote the following after her death: "The deceased lady was a militant Radical, but she lived only to do good ... Her whole life was wrapped up in trying to elevate the poor, and alleviate the sufferings of all that were downtrodden."

Contributors
or BIOS ON THE BAYOU

Ali Arnold rarely crosses Canal Street. Instead, she divides her time between the Lakefront where she teaches English at the University of New Orleans and the Marigny where she shares a shotgun with her nineteen-year-old cat, Simon. You're just as likely, though, to find her on a dance floor on Frenchmen Street where she's learning to swing out to that trad jazz.

Barbara Bodichon (1827-1891) was an English feminist, writer and painter. She was one of the founders of the women's movement in England, fighting for suffrage, for the right to work and for economic equality within marriage, among other causes. In art, she specialized in English landscapes, and, apparently, did some sketches of the outskirts of New Orleans. (If they exist, we would love to publish them.) She visited the US, with her

Sandra Burshell is a New Orleans photographer and visual artist who uses her photographs as ends in themselves as well as a source for inspiration for her pastels and oils. After Hurricane Katrina, through her photographs, she sought to find beauty and humanity in the devastation, on an individual rather than the panoramic scale. Some of these photographs were exhibited in "Katrina Exposed," New Orleans Museum of Art, 2006, and are in the museum's permanent collection. Her pastels exhibit the same sensitivity and attention to light, shadow and composition. For more information: www.sandraburshell.com

Sarah DeBacher lives with her husband and their many cats in a renovated shotgun in the historic Holy Cross neighborhood of the Lower Ninth Ward. She teaches writing at the University of New Orleans and in New Orleans' Recovery School District's high schools for the Bard Early College Program.

Lolis Eric Elie is a writer and filmmaker. Born and raised in New Orleans, he co-produced the documentary *Faubourg Treme* and works as a staff writer for the HBO series, *Treme*. For 14 years, he was a metro columnist for *The Times-Picayune*.

Mark Folse lives and writes on Toulouse Street in New Orleans, the city to which he returned following the city's flooding after a twenty-year absence. His work has appeared in the anthologies *The Maple Leaf Rag IV* and *Finn Mc-Cool's Chronicles 2009*, the forthcoming *A Howling in the Wires* collection, which he co-edited, *The Dead Mule School of Southern Literature*, *The Times-Picayune* and his own collection *Carry Me Home: A Journey Back to New Orleans* (Lulu, 2008). He never seems to find a lack of things to write about at his blog Toulouse Street — Odd Bits of Life in New Orleans (http://toulousestreet.net).

Rebecca Freeland-Hebert was born and raised in sunny Alberta. She packed up her dog and came to New Orleans to study God, love and death. Having chosen tattooing as a form of her own expression, she saw God, love and death in the Katrina tattoos of New Orleanians.

She is currently finishing her theology degree in Alberta and awaiting the arrival of her first child with her husband Eric.

Anne Gisleson is chair of the writing program at the New Orleans Center for Creative Arts (NOCCA), Louisiana's arts conservatory for high-school students. Her writing has appeared in various places including the *Oxford American*, *The New Orleans Review* and *Best American Non-Required Reading*. She also helps run Press Street, a nonprofit which promotes art and literature in the community through events, publications and art education.

Kris Lackey is the author of *Road-Frames: The American Highway Narrative* and short fiction in *Missouri Review*, *Wisconsin Review* and other magazines. He teaches at the University of New Orleans.

When **Sarah Inman's** not hanging upside down, hula hooping or chasing after her son, she writes. She is the author of *The Least Resistance* (NOLAFugees Press, 2010) and *Finishing Skills* (Livingston Press, 2005).

Sam Jasper lives in the Marigny in New Orleans, a district that shelters other malcontents and those with an artistic bent. Sam was a contributor to *Louisiana in Words* (Pelican Press 2007), is a contributor at the

Back of Town blog, as well as erratically keeping the New Orleans Slate blog updated. Sam's archived pieces written just after Katrina can be found at the Katrina Refrigerator blog. Sam is also the co-editor of *A Howling in the Wires*, a collection of pieces about post-Katrina New Orleans, due out August 2010.

Jennifer A. Kuchta teaches creative writing, literature and composition at the University of New Orleans. Her nonfiction can be found in *Year Zero: A Year of Reporting From Post-Katrina New Orleans* and *Soul is Bulletproof: Reports From Reconstruction New Orleans* while her fiction has appeared most recently in *Life in the Wake: Fiction From Post-Katrina New Orleans*. Kuchta still makes her home in Uptown, New Orleans, with a four-pack of rescue dogs.

Rex Noone is an expert in so many fields that it becomes redundant. He is the offspring of the gods Bacchus and Nihilia, the sacred gods of grapes and grapelessness, respectively. He considers the short story that he wrote for *Do You Know What It Means To Miss New Orleans?* – "Professor Stevens Goes to Mardi Gras" – to be by far the most eloquent piece in the anthology. After dark, he has been known to declare, at varying degrees of volume and clarity, "My knowledge abounds!" – or is it "My NOLA's unsound"? Either way, the pentameter bewilders those who wake to it. He is currently underemployed.

Matt Phelan is a New Orleans born graphic designer and multimedia artist who believes fully in appreciating this great city before a combination of mother nature's fury and man's negligence cause its eventual demise. He is a founding member of the 5th Quarter Allstars, an Elder Beardmaster with the Church of His Holy Beard, a community organizer for Leash Your Children and the creator of the not-for-much-profit KetchingUp.org.

Reggie J. Poché, a tenth-generation Louisianian, teaches creative writing, technical writing and composition at the University of New Orleans. His most recent fiction has appeared in *Ginger Hill*, *Zahir*, *Margin* and *River Styx*. In 2006, he won the Margery McKinney Short Fiction Prize and was nominated for the Pushcart Prize and Best New American Voices. He is currently at work on a novel, tentatively titled *Antediluvian Men*.

David Rutledge is a teacher of English at the University of New Orleans. His book on Vladimir Nabokov will be published next year by McFarland Press. He is also the co-editor and a contributor to *Do You Know What It Means To*

Miss New Orleans? The book release party at the Saturn Bar, in February of 2006, was the most remarkable evening in his eleven years of evenings in New Orleans. Thanks to all who were there.

Tracey Tangerine is the author of *Buddy Zooka in the French Quarter and Beyond* (Chin Music Press 2010). That novel has been called "[t]he best New Orleans story ever written" — at least it says that on the second page of the book. It is a riotous romp of a young musician and his many adventures. It also has a very relevant theme of environmental awareness.

Eve Troeh worked as a radio and print journalist in New Orleans before and after Hurricane Katrina. Her stories have been heard on National Public Radio, American Public Media and various other programs across the country. Her last project in New Orleans was the audio documentary "Finding Solid Ground," produced with Molly Peterson. Eve moved to Los Angeles in 2007, where she continues to report and produce for radio. She thought she'd live in New Orleans forever.

Charles Dudley Warner (1829-1900) wrote many works, including essays, novels and, along with Mark Twain, *The Gilded Age* (1873). One of the two writers coined that famous phrase, "gilded age," thereby labeling an era for posterity. Warner wrote and traveled extensively and should not be reduced to a few famous quotations. Nonetheless, he coined, "Politics makes strange bedfellows," and, "Everybody talks about the weather, but nobody does anything about it." He also edited a forty-five volume work entitled *The World's Best Literature: Ancient and Modern* (1896). Wow. In *The Whims of Travel* (1875), he wrote, "The best thing about traveling is going home."

Thanks to Chance Sweat, for his work and enthusiasm; he helped in many ways, from research to proofreading, always doing a top-rate job.

Thanks also to the English Department at the University of New Orleans for assigning Mr. Sweat to be my research assistant for one semester.

Thanks to Governor Bobby Jindal for not having budgeted our university out of existence, yet. Thanks for squeezing us to point of passing out. Keep squeezing, Bobby. No one knows his real reason for cutting education to the bone. My guess is that only the uneducated vote for him.

Who benefits by having a less educated populace?

Acknowledgments & Anger

Perhaps those who need to look up the word "populace." Pander to them, Piyush.

The University of New Orleans is one of the most underrated universities in this nation. We provide an excellent education to over thirteen thousand students, as of 2010. This university is necessary to the city. To our home.

They are cutting us. They are trying to wash us away. We should not stand for it.

We teachers don't earn enough to raise a family. And guess what — that is not what we are complaining about. We are complaining about the threat to the existence of our city's university. Don't tell me it's a budget thing, when there are thirteen thousand students and I make less than a Bourbon Street bartender.

Don't be fooled by Jindal's oil cleanup speeches. Yes, he is having his Giuliani moment, but deep down he is as bad as those oil execs who are willing to ruin the Gulf. All one has to do is look at what he has already done to our university, the hiring freeze, the increased class sizes, the horrible reduced staff. He *is* our BP.

May the University of New Orleans someday receive the respect that it deserves. May the governor wake up one day and realize that educated people are necessary to build successful levees, to prevent oil spills, to prevent the next man-made disaster. Education is necessary to keeping New Orleans and Louisiana as safe as possible.

We need more brains in this state.

Our student body represents the people of New Orleans, from Versailles to West End, from the Lower Ninth to Black Pearl, from Algiers to Lakeshore. Let us save our neighborhood; let us educate our neighbors.

A great city needs an excellent and well-funded city university. That should not even be a question.

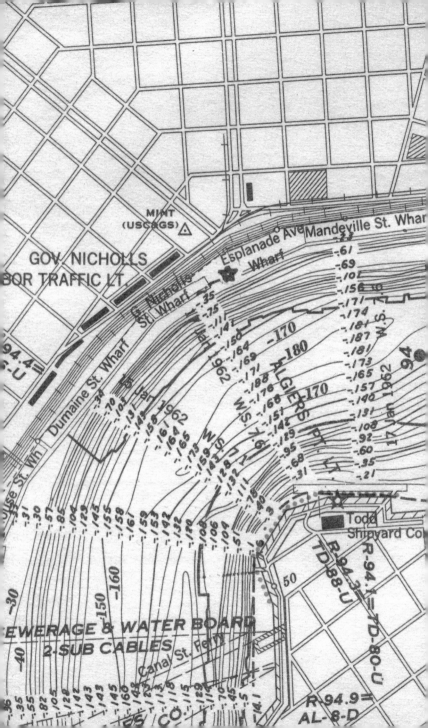

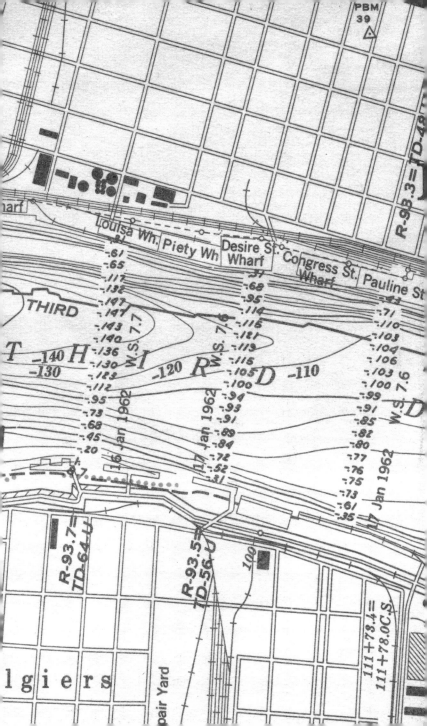

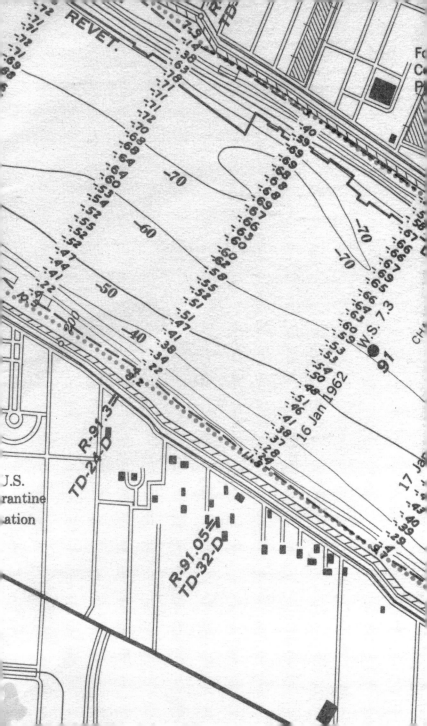

LA.

SOUTHE

△ CHALMETTE
MONUMENT
(USC&GS)

CHALMETTE OBSTRUCTION LT.

R-90.3
TD-56-D

R-90.1
TD-64-D.

R-89.9
TD-72-D

.77
.55
.59
.62
.62
.63
.64
.65
.66

.45
.59
.62
.62
.63
.63
.62
.63
.63
.60
.61

.36
.46
.57
.58
.59
.60

.50

1962 W.S. 7.3
.52
.57
.55

90

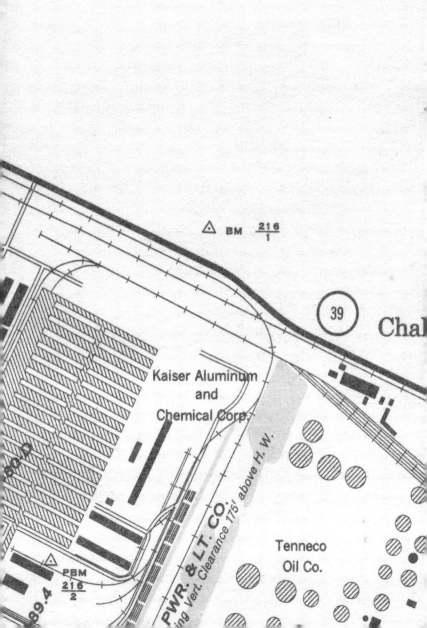

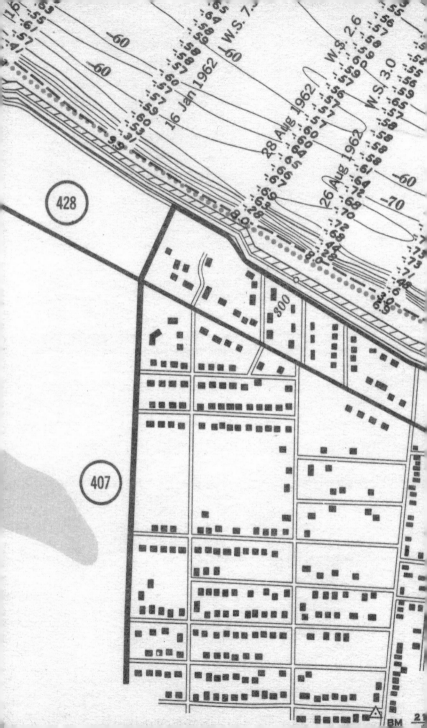

CAT ISLAND

HORN ISLAND

PETIT BOIS ISL.

Light House

SHIP ISLAND

ISLE AU PIED

FLATBOAT I.

Elephant Pass

MARTIN ISLAND

MITCHELLS I.

INT COMFORT I.

CHANDELEUR SOUND

CHANDELEUR ISLAND

NORTH Is.

G U L F

CHANDELEUR SOUND

ERROL ISLAND

O F

SOUND

BRETON ISLAND

M E X I C O

an Pass

Beu Ronde

North Pass

Pass à Loutre

North East Pass

Garden Is.

South East Pass

Port Eads